BEYOND THE TENTH gives advice and teachings on the care of man's physical and spiritual forms. Preparation on the present plane of existence can equip man more fully for the life which commences in the Astral World.

BEYOND THE TENTH is a book that will bring comfort and learning to many—but especially to those who are students and disciples of T. Lobsang Rampa.

Also by T. LOBSANG RAMPA

THE THIRD EYE
DOCTOR FROM LHASA
THE RAMPA STORY
THE CAVE OF THE ANCIENTS
LIVING WITH THE LAMA
YOU-FOREVER
WISDOM OF THE ANCIENTS
THE SAFFRON ROBE
CHAPTERS OF LIFE

and published by CORGI BOOKS

T. Lobsang Rampa

Beyond the Tenth

TRANSWORLD PUBLISHERS LTD
A National General Company

BEYOND THE TENTH

A CORGI BOOK 552 08105 1

First publication in Great Britain

PRINTING HISTORY

Corgi Edition published 1969
Corgi Edition reprinted 1969
Corgi Edition reprinted 1970

Copyright © T. Lobsang Rampa 1969

This book is set in Baskerville 11 pt.

Corgi Books are published by Transworld Publishers, Ltd., Cavendish House; 57–59 Uxbridge Road, Ealing, London, W.5

Made and printed in Great Britain by
Richard Clay (The Chaucer Press), Ltd., Bungay, Suffolk

Dedicated to —

those loyal and constant Readers who have stuck by me throughout the years, even in the face of press campaigns; to those whom I now regard as friends.

To YOU

of course, who else?

THE TITLE

To save a lot of later questions, let me say now that Man is one tenth conscious, the other nine tenths deal with the sub-conscious and all that which comes under the heading 'Racial Memories' and the Occult.

This book is about YOU, not just about one tenth of you, but also that which goes
            Beyond the Tenth.

A SPECIAL LETTER

Dear Reader,

For over a decade you have been writing to me from all over the world, even from the other side of the Iron Curtain, writing to me some thirty or forty letters a day, letters which I have conscientiously answered. But quite a number of you have written to say that an Author of books such as mine belongs to the Reader, saying that an Author such as I cannot end with nine books but must go on writing until reasonable questions are answered.

To that I replied by writing to several representative people with this question; 'Well, what DO you want in the tenth book? Tell me, tell me what you want, tell me what I've missed in other books, and I will write that tenth book.'

So as a result of the letters I have received in answer to my questions, I have written this book which you are about to read.

Some of you, no doubt, will say that it is repetition here and there. I can only reply that it is the unanimous request of my 'Panel of Readers' or it would not be in this book, and if you think it is repetitious in places, well, it might serve to refresh your memory.

One question I am asked in particular is, 'Oh, Dr. Rampa, visit me in the astral, cure me of this, cure me of that, tell me who is going to win the Irish Sweepstake, come along to our Group Meeting in the astral.' But these readers forget that there are only 24 hours in each day; they also forget the difference in time zones, etc., etc. Even more important, they forget that although I, in the astral, can see them clearly when I want to, yet they may not always be able to see me, although an astonishing number of people have written to me confirming exactly astral visits, telepathic contacts, etc.

Well, it's not intended that this shall be a long letter, so let us get on with the book itself, shall we?

T. LOBSANG RAMPA

CHAPTER ONE

The soft summer night sighed gently, and whispered quietly to the nodding willows fringing the Serpent Temple. Faint ripples undulated across the placid lake as some early-rising fish sought the surface in search of unwary insects. Above the hard, high mountain peaks, with the everlasting spume of snow flying banner-wise from it, a solitary star shone with glittering brilliance in the luminescent sky.

In the granaries faint squeaks and rustles betrayed the presence of hungry mice foraging in the barley barrels. Stealthy footsteps and two glaring eyes as Watchman Cat appeared on the scene brought a scuffle of scurrying mice and then utter silence. Watchman Cat sniffed around suspiciously, then, satisfied, jumped to a low window and sat looking out at the fast-approaching dawn.

Flickering butter-lamps hissed and spat and momentarily flared brighter as night-duty acolytes replenished their supplies. From some inner temple came a subdued murmur and the tiny tinkle of different silver bells. Out upon a high roof a solitary figure stood to greet the coming dawn, hands already clasped about the neck of the Morning Call trumpet.

Shadowy, indistinct figures appeared at some back entrance and gathered to march down the mountain trail towards a small tributary of the Happy River from whence came the water supply for the needs of the Potala. Aged men, husky men, and mere wisps of boys, members of the Serving Class, marched in age-old procession down the mountain-side carrying hard leather pails to dip in the river and then laboriously manhandle up to the kitchens and storage tanks.

The downward trip was easy, a half-awake throng still bemusedly thinking of the joys of sleep. By the little well, so constantly filled by the tributary, they stood awhile chatting, exchanging gossip gleaned from the kitchens the day before. Lounging, killing time, postponing the inevitable and hard climb up the mountain-side.

Overhead night had already given way to the approaching day. The purple curtain of night had fled to the West before the advancing dawn, the sky no longer showed the brilliant, hard pinpoints of light which were the stars in their courses, but instead was luminous with the rays of the approaching sun striking through the lower levels and lighting up the undersides of the slight alto-stratus clouds which scurried above. The mountain peaks were now tinged with gold, a white gold which threw rainbows from the blowing snow at the peak heads, and which made each mountain top appear as if it were a living fountain of iridescent colour.

Swiftly the light advanced and the Valley of Lhasa, hitherto in the purple shadows of the night, lit up, great flashing gleams shone from the golden roofs of the Potala and reflected also from the Jo Kang Cathedral in Lhasa City. At the foot of the Potala near the coloured carvings a little group of early risers gazed up in awe at the scintillating lights above them, thinking that it must be a reflection of the spirit of the Inmost One.

At the foot of our mountain path, however, the serving monks, quite immune to the glories of nature, stood chatting, killing time before taking up their burdens and proceeding uphill. The old monk, Big Ears, stood upon a flat rock and gazed out across the lake and the nearby river; 'Did you hear what the traders were saying in the city yesterday?' he asked a younger monk standing beside him.

'No,' replied the younger one, 'but the traders always have wonderful tales to tell. What did you hear, Old One?'

Old Big Ears worked his jaws around a bit and wiped his nose on the end of his robe. Then he spat expertly and with precision between two filled buckets. 'I had to go into the city yesterday,' he said, 'and there in the Street of Shops I chanced upon some traders displaying their wares. One of them seemed to be a knowledgeable sort of man, just like me, in fact, so I tarried in my task and talked to him.' He stopped a moment and chewed around his jaws again, and looked at the rippling water. Somewhere in the distance a small acolyte had thrown a pebble and hit a frog, and now the frog was croaking in astonished complaint. 'A knowledgeable man he was, a man who had travelled to many strange parts. He told me that once he left his homeland of India and travelled across the great waters to Merikee. I told him that I had to see about new buckets because some of ours were worn out, and he said that in Merikee no one had to carry buckets of water up a mountain path. Everyone has water in their houses, he said, it runs through pipes. They have a special room, where they get a lot of water, called a bathroom.'

The younger monk started with surprise and said, 'Water in their houses, eh? And in a special room too, eh? That sounds too marvellous to be true, I wish we had something like it here. But of course you can't believe all these travellers' tales. I once heard a trader telling me that in some lands they have light as bright as lightning which they keep in glass bottles and it turns the night into day.' He shook his head as if he could hardly believe the things he had heard, and the old monk, Big Ears, afraid that he was going to be ousted as the teller of tales, resumed, 'Yes, in the land of Merikee they have many wonderful things. This water, it is in every house. You turn a piece of metal and the water comes gushing out, hot or cold, whichever you want, as much as you want, whenever you want. It's a great miracle, by Buddha's Tooth,' he said. 'I certainly would like some other way of getting water up to the kitchens. Many a long year I've been doing this, carrying and carrying water and nothing but water, I feel that I've walked my feet and my legs right down to the knees and I've got a permanent tilt to the side through fighting against the mountain's pull. Still, water in every room? No, it is not possible!'

Together they lapsed into silence, and then started into alertness as down the path strode one of the Guardians of our Law, the Proctors. The immense man strode along, and each one of the monks found urgent business to attend to. One poured out his pail of water and refilled it, another picked up two pails and hurried up, striding along the mountain path. Soon all the monks were on the move, carting water, the first round of the water carriers for the day. The Proctor gazed around for a few moments, then he too made his way up the mountain path after them.

Silence, comparative silence, fell upon the scene, disturbed only by faint chanting from the mountain top above and by the sleepy protests of some bird who thought it was rather too early to get up and go about the business of the day.

Old Mrs. MacDunnigan cackled as if she had just laid an oversize egg and turned to her friend Mrs. O'Flannigan. 'No more of these lectures for me,' she said, 'telling us that the priests of Tibet can do telepathy. What nonsense! What will they ask us to believe next?'

Mrs. O'Flannigan snorted like a Salvation Army

trumpeter at his best and remarked, 'Why can't they use telephones like the rest of us, that's what I want to know!'

So the two ladies went their way unaware that they were 'the other side of the coin'; monks in Tibet could not believe houses could have running water in rooms and the two Western women could not believe that priests of Tibet could telepathise.

But are we not all like that? CAN we see 'the other fellow's' point of view? Do we realise that what is commonplace HERE is the strangest of strange THERE —and vice versa?

Our first request is about life after death, or death, or contact with those who have left this life. First of all let us deal with a person who is leaving this Earth. The person is very, very sick usually, and 'death' follows as a result of the breakdown of the human body mechanism. The body becomes untenable, inoperable, it becomes a clay case enshrouding the immortal spirit which cannot bear such restraint, so the immortal spirit leaves. When it has left the dead body, when it has left the familiar confines of the Earth, the—what shall we call it? Soul, Overself, Spirit, or what? Let's call it Soul this time for a change—the Soul, then, is in strange surroundings where there are many more senses and faculties than those experienced on Earth. Here on Earth we have to clomp around, or sit in a tin box which we call a car, but unless we are rich enough to pay airfares we are earthbound. Not so when we are out of the body, because when out of the body, when in this new dimension which we will call 'the astral world', we can travel at will and instantly by thought, we do not have to wait for a bus or a train, we are not hampered by a car nor by an aeroplane where one waits longer in a waiting room than one spends on the actual journey.

In the astral we can travel at any speed we will.

'We will' is a deliberate pair of words, because we actually 'will' the speed at which we travel, the height and the route. If, for example, you want to enjoy the wondrous scenery of the astral world with its verdant pastures and its lushly stocked lakes, we can drift as light as thistledown just above the land, just above the water, or we can rise higher and soar over the astral mountain tops.

When we are in this new and wonderful dimension we are experiencing so many changes that unless we are very careful we tend to forget those who mourn us on that awful old ball of Earth which we have so recently left, we tend to forget, but if people on Earth mourn us too fervently then we feel inexplicable twinges and pulls, and strange feelings of sorrow and sadness. Any of you who have neuritis or chronic toothache will know what it's like; you get a sudden vicious jerk at a nerve which nearly lifts you out of the chair. In the same way, when we are in the astral world and a person is mourning us with deep lamentation, instead of getting on with their own affairs, they hinder us, they provide unwanted 'anchors' which retard our progress.

Let us go just a little beyond our first days in the astral, let us go to the time when we have entered the Hall of Memories, when we have decided what work we are going to do in the astral, how we are going to help others, how we are going to learn ourselves, let us imagine that we are busy at our task of helping or learning and then just imagine a hand jerking at the back of our neck—tweak, tweak, tweak, and pull, pull, pull—it distracts the attention, it makes learning hard, it makes helping others very difficult because we cannot add our full concentration or attention to that which we should be doing because of the insistent tug and interference caused by those mourning us upon the Earth.

Many people seem to think that they can get in

touch with those who have 'passed over' by going to a backstreet medium, paying a few dollars or a few shillings and just getting a message like having a telephone answered by an intermediary. Well, even this telephone business; try telephoning Spain from Canada! Try telephoning England from Uruguay!! First you have the difficulty that the intermediary, that is the telephone operator on Earth, or the medium, is not familiar with the circumstances, may even be not very familiar with the language in which we desire to speak. And then there are all sorts of hisses, clicks, and clunks on the wire, reception may be difficult, reception, in fact, is often impossible. Yet here on Earth we know the telephone number we desire to call, but who is going to tell you the telephone number of a person who recently left the Earth and now lives in the astral world? A telephone number in the astral world? Well, near enough, because every person on every world has a personal frequency, a personal wavelength. In just the same way as the B.B.C. radio stations, or the Voice of America stations in the U.S.A. have their own frequencies, so do people have frequencies, and if we know those frequencies we can tune-in to the radio station PROVIDED atmospheric conditions are suitable, the time of the day is correct, and the station is actually broadcasting. It is not possible to tune-in and be infallibly sure that you can receive a station for the simple reason that something may have put them out of action.

It is the same with people who have passed beyond this life. You may be able to get in touch with them if you know their basic personal frequency, and if they are able to receive a telepathic message on that frequency. For the most part, unless a medium is very, very experienced indeed, he or she can be led astray by some nuisance-entities who are playing at being humans and who can pick up the thoughts of what the 'caller' wants.

That is, supposing Mrs. Brown, a new widow, wants to get in touch with Mr. Brown, a newly-freed human who has escaped to the Other Side, one of these lesser entities who are not humans can perceive what she wants to ask Mr. Brown, can perceive from Mrs. Brown's thoughts how Mr. Brown spoke, what he looked like. So the entity, like a naughty schoolboy who didn't get the discipline that he sadly needed, can influence the well-meaning medium by giving her a description of Mr. Brown which has just been obtained from the mind of Mrs. Brown. The medium will give 'startling proof' by describing in detail the appearance of Mr. Brown who is 'standing by me now'. Well, the very experienced person cannot be deceived in that way, but the very experienced person is few and far between, and just does not have time to deal with such things. Furthermore, when commerce comes into it, when a person demands such-and-such a sum for a mediumistic sitting, a lower vibration is brought into the proceedings and a genuine message is thus all too frequently prevented.

It is unkind and unfair to let your sorrows harm and handicap a person who has left the Earth and who is now working elsewhere. After all, supposing you were very busy at some important task, and supposing some other person whom you could not see kept jerking at the nape of your neck and prodding you, and blaring silly thoughts into your ears, your concentration would go and you really would call down all sorts of unkind thoughts upon your tormentor. Be sure that if you really love the person who has left the Earth, and if that person really loves you, you will meet again because you will be attracted together when you also leave the Earth. In the astral world you cannot meet a person whom you hate or who hates you, it just cannot be done because that would disrupt the harmony of the astral world and that cannot be. Of course, if you are doing astral travel you can go to the LOWER astral which is, one might say, the waiting room or entrance to the real astral world. In the lower astral one can discuss differences with some heat, but in the higher regions —no.

So remember this; if you really love the other person and the other person really loves you, you will be together again but on a very different footing. There will be none of the misunderstandings as upon this Earth, one cannot tell lies in the astral world because in that world everyone can see the aura, and if an astral-dweller tells a lie then anyone in sight knows about it immediately because of the discord which appears in his personal vibrations and in the colours of the aura. So one learns to be truthful.

People seem to have the idea that unless they have a lavish funeral for the departed and go into ecstasies of sorrow, they are not showing a proper appreciation of the deceased. But that is not the case; mourning is selfish, mourning causes grave interference and disturbance to the person newly arrived in the astral plane. Mourning, in fact, could really be regarded as self-pity, sorrow for oneself that one has lost a person who did so much for those left behind. It is better and shows greater respect and thought to control grief and avoid hysterical outbursts which cause such distress to people who have really left.

The astral worlds (yes, definitely plural!) are very real. Things are as real and as substantial upon those worlds as they appear to us to be here on this Earth, actually they appear more substantial because there are extra senses, extra abilities, extra colours, and extra sounds. We can do so much more in the astral state. But——

'Dr. Rampa, you have told us so much about the astral world in your books, but you haven't told us enough. What do people do, what do they eat, how do they occupy their time? Can't you tell us this?'

Most certainly I can tell you because I have eidetic memory, that is, I can remember everything that ever happened to me. I can remember dying and being born, and I have the great advantage that I can astral travel when fully conscious. So let us look at this matter of the astral worlds and what one does.

In the first case there is not just one astral world, but many, as many in fact as there are different vibrations of people. Perhaps the best way of realising this is by considering radio; in radio there are many, many different radio stations in all parts of the world. If those stations tried to share a common wavelength or frequency there would be bedlam, everyone would interfere with everyone else, and so radio stations each have their own separate frequency, and if you want the B.B.C., London, you tune-in to those frequencies allotted to the B.B.C. If you want Moscow you tune-in to the frequencies allotted to Moscow. There are thousands of different radio stations, each with their own frequency, each a separate entity not interfering with the others.

In the same way astral worlds are different planes of existence having different frequencies, so that upon astral world X, for example, you will get all people who are compatible within certain limits. In astral world Y you will find another set of people who are compatible within their own limits. Lower down, in what we call the lower astral, there are conditions somewhat the same as on the Earth, that is there are mixed types of people, and the average person who gets out of his body during the hours of sleep and goes astral travelling, he goes to that lower astral where all entities may mix. The lower astral, then, is a meeting place for people of different races and different creeds, and even from different worlds. It is very similar to life upon Earth.

As we progress higher we find the frequencies becoming purer and purer. Whereas in the lower astral you can have an argument with a person and tell him you hate the sight of him if you want to, when you get higher in the astral planes you cannot, because you cannot get people who are opposed to each other. So remember that the astral worlds are like radio stations with different frequencies, or, if you wish, like a big school with different classrooms, each succeeding class being higher in vibration than the one before, so that class or grade One is a common denominator class, or astral world, where all may meet while the process of assessing their capacities goes on. Then as they do their allotted tasks—we shall deal with that in a moment—they become raised higher and higher until eventually they pass out of the astral plane of worlds altogether and enter into a state where there is no longer rebirth, reincarnation, and where people now deal with much higher forms of being than humans.

But you want to know what happens when you die. Well, actually I have told you a lot about it in my previous books. You leave your body and your astral form floats off and goes to the lower astral, where it recovers from shocks and harm caused by living or dying conditions on Earth. Then, after a few days according to Earth time reckoning, one sees all one's past in the Hall of Memories, sees what one has accomplished and what one has failed to accomplish, and by assessing the successes or failures one can decide on what has to be learned in the future, that is, shall one reincarnate again right away, or shall one spend perhaps six hundred years in the astral. It all depends on what a person has to learn, it depends on one's purpose in the scale of evolution. But I've told you all about that in previous books. Let me mention another subject for a moment before saying what people do in the astral world.

A very pleasant lady wrote to me and said, 'I am so frightened. I am so frightened that I shall die alone with no one to help me, no one to direct me in the Path that I should take. You, in Tibet, had the Lamas who directed the consciousness of a dying person. I have no one and I am so frightened.'

That is not correct, you know. No one is alone, no one has 'no one'. You may think you are alone, and quite possibly there is no one near your earthly body, yet in the astral there are very special helpers who await by the deathbed so that just as soon as the astral form starts to separate from the dying physical body the helpers are there to give every assistance, just as in the case of a birth there are people waiting to deliver the new-born baby. Death to Earth is birth into the astral world, and the necessary trained attendants are there to provide their specialised services, so there is no need for fear, there should never be fear. Remember that when the time comes, as it comes to all of us, for you to pass from this world of sorrows, there will be people on the Other Side waiting for you, caring for you, and helping you in precisely the same manner that there are people on Earth awaiting the birth of a new baby.

When the helpers have this astral body which has just been separated from the dead physical, they treat it carefully and help it with a knowledge of where it is. Many people who have not been prepared think they are in Heaven or Hell. The helpers tell them exactly where they are, they help them to adjust, they show them the Hall of Memories, and they care for the newcomer as they, in their turn, have been cared for.

This matter of Hell—there is no such thing, you know, Hell was actually a place of judgement near Jerusalem, Hell was a small village near two very high rocks and between the rocks and extending for some distance around was a quaking bog which sent up gouts of sulphurous vapours, a bog that was always drenched in the stench of burning brimstone. In those far-off days a person who was accused of a crime was taken to this village and 'went through Hell'. He was placed at one end of the bog and was told of the crimes of which he had been accused, he was told that if he could cross the bog unharmed he was innocent, but if he failed and was swallowed by the bog he was guilty. Then the accused was goaded into action—perhaps a soldier poked him in a delicate part with a spear—anyway, the poor wretch ran 'through Hell', through all the swirling fog of sulphur and brimstone fumes, along the path surrounded by boiling pitch, where the earth quaked and shook, inspiring terror in the strongest, and if he reached the other side he had passed through the valley of Hell and had been purged of any offence and was innocent again. So don't believe that you will go to Hell. You won't because there is no such thing. God, no matter what we call Him, is a God of kindness, a God of compassion. No one is ever condemned, no one is ever sentenced to eternal damnation, there are no such things as devils who jump up and down on one and plunge pitch forks into one's shuddering body. That is all a figment in the imagination of crazed priests who tried to gain dominance over the bodies and souls of those who knew no better. There is only hope and knowledge that if one works for it, one can atone for any crime, no matter how bad that crime seems to have been. So—no one is ever 'extinguished', no one is ever abandoned by God. Most people fear death because they have a murky conscience, and these priests who should know better have taught about hell-fire and eternal torment, eternal damnation and all that, and the poor wretched person who has heard those stories thinks that immediately he dies he is going to be seized by devils and horrendous things wreaked upon him. Don't believe it, don't believe it at all. I remember all, and I can go to the astral at any time, and I repeat, there is no such thing as Hell, there is no such thing as eternal torment, there is always redemption, there is always another chance, there is always mercy, compassion, and understanding. Those who say that there is Hell and torment, well, they are not right in the head, they are sadists or something, and they are not worthy of another thought.

We fear to die for that reason and for another; we fear to die because the fear is planted in us. If people remembered the glories of the astral world they would want to go there in droves, they wouldn't want to stay on this Earth any longer, they would want to shirk their classes, they would want to commit suicide, and suicide is a very bad thing, you know, it hurts oneself. It doesn't hurt anyone else, but one becomes one of life's drop-out's when one commits suicide. Think of it like this; if you are training to be a professional person of some kind, a lawyer or a doctor, well, you have to study and you have to pass examinations, but if you lose heart half way through you drop out of your course and then you do not become a lawyer or a doctor, and before you can become a lawyer or a doctor you have to cease being a drop-out and get back into the class and study all over again. And by that time you find the curriculum has changed, there are different textbooks, and all you have learnt before becomes useless, so you start at the bottom again. Thus it is that if you commit suicide, well, you have to come back, you reincarnate again, which is just the same as entering college for another course, but you reincarnate again and you learn all the lessons all over again right from the start, and all you learnt before is now obsolete, so you've wasted a lifetime, haven't you? Don't commit suicide, it's never, never, never worth it.

Well, that has taken us quite away from what people do in the astral. A lot depends on the state of evolution of the person, a lot of it depends on what that person is preparing for. But the astral worlds are very, very beautiful places, there is wonderful scenery with colours not even dreamed of upon the Earth, there is music, a music not even dreamed of upon the Earth, there are houses, but each person can build his or her house by thought. You think it, and if you think hard enough, it is. In the same way, when you get to the astral world first you are quite naked just as you are when you come to the Earth, and then you think what sort of clothes you are going to wear; you don't have to wear clothes, but most people do for some strange reason, and one can see the most remarkable collection of garments because each person makes their own clothes according to any style they are thinking about. In the same way, they build their houses in any style they are thinking about. There are no cars, of course, and no buses, and no trains, you don't need them. Why be cluttered by a car when you can move as fast as you wish by wishing? So, by thought power alone you can visit any part of the astral world.

In the astral there are many jobs that one can do. You can be a helper to those who are every second arriving from the Earth, you can do nursing, you can do healing, because many of those who arrive from the Earth are not aware of the reality of the astral and they believe whatever their religion has taught them to believe. Or, if they are atheists they believe in nothing, and so they are enshrouded in a black, black fog, a fog that is sticky and confusing, and until they can acquire some sort of understanding that they are blinded by their own folly they cannot be helped much, so attendants follow them around and try to break away the fog. Then there are those who counsel the astral people who have to return to Earth. Where do they want to go, what sort of parents do they want, what sort of family conditions, a rich family or a poor family? What sort of conditions will enable them to do the tasks which they plan to do? It all looks so easy when in the astral world, but it is not always so easy when one is on the Earth, you know.

In the lower astral people often eat, they can smoke also if they want to! Whatever they want to eat is actually manufactured from the atmosphere by thought, not so amazing when you think of prana which is believed in implicitly on Earth. So you can eat what you wish, you can drink what you wish also, but actually all that is just folly because one is acquiring all the energy, all the sustenance from the atmospheric radiations and eating and drinking is just a habit. One soon shucks off those habits and is the better for it. You can take it, then, that one does much the same in the lower astral as one does upon the Earth.

Yes, Mrs. So-and-So, there is a sex life in the astral as well, but it is far, far better than anything you can ever experience on the Earth because you have such an enhanced range of sensations. So if you have not had much of a balanced sex life on Earth remember that in the astral you will have, because it is necessary to make a balanced person.

Of course the higher one rises in the astral worlds, that is the more one increases one's personal vibrations, then the better the experiences, the more pleasant they become, and the more satisfying the whole existence becomes.

Many people on Earth are all members of a group. You may have, for example (and for example only) ten people who together really complete one astral entity. On the Earth we have these ten people, and perhaps three, four, five, or six die; well, the person who is in the astral does not become really complete until all the group are united. It is very difficult explaining such a thing because it involves different dimensions which are not even known upon this Earth, but you have felt a remarkable affinity with a certain person, a person who, of course, is absolutely separate from you, you may have thought how compatible you were with that person, you may feel a sense of loss when that person goes away. Well, quite possibly that person is a member of your group and when you die to this Earth you will be united together as one entity. Upon the Earth all these people are like tentacles reaching out to get different sensations, different experiences during that brief flickering of consciousness which comprises a lifetime upon Earth. Yet when all the members of that group—when all the tentacles—are pulled in, one has in effect the experience of perhaps ten lifetimes in one. One has to come to Earth to learn the hard material things because there are no such experiences in the astral world.

Not everyone is a member of a group, you know, but you probably know whole groups of people who just cannot manage without each other. It may be members of a big family, they are always dashing around to see how the others are doing, and even when they marry they still have to forsake their partners at times and rush back home as if they are all going in like a lot of chickens under the old hen! Many people are individualists, not members of a group upon the Earth, they have come to do certain things alone, and they rise or fall by their own efforts on the Earth. The poor souls often have a very bad time indeed upon the Earth, and it doesn't necessarily mean that they have immense kharmic debts because they get suffering, it means that they are doing special work and incurring good kharma for a few lives to come.

Really experienced people can tell what other people have been in a past life, but don't believe the advertisement you read where, for a small sum of money, you can have all your past incarnations told. Don't believe that for a moment because most of these people who make such claims are fakes. If they demand money for such a service, then you can be sure that they are fakes, because the really trained person does not take money for these occult purposes as it lowers the personal vibrations! It is such a tragic thing that so many advertisements appear which are arrant fakes. People flit about examining the Akashic Record or looking into the past to see what you did wrong, or looking a bit forward to see what you did right, provided you pay enough money. And then all these cults who teach you the Mystery of the Ages provided you pay a monthly sum for the rest of your life. Some of these are just ordinary commercial correspondence colleges, they want your money, possibly they might do you some good—they might teach you not to believe all advertisements, for example. But my own point of view is this; if a person advertises in glamorous terms what he or she can do for you for a small outlay, well, be suspicious. If these people could do it they would do it for themselves and get money and power that way. The fact that they have to run a correspondence course or do this or that service, makes them, in my opinion, suspect, and I sincerely wish that there was some way in which these advertisements could be censored and controlled. There are many, many people who are utterly genuine, but my own personal experience is that it is rare indeed for such a person to advertise. Remember also that people who make these wondrous claims about how they go into the astral for you and look at all your records, etc., etc., well, you can't prove them really wrong, can you, just the same as you can't prove them right. So, just to be on the safe side, it is far better not to bother with people who advertise as such, but instead meditate, because if you meditate you can get the results you want. You know yourself better than any other person, and most assuredly you know yourself better than a person who is going to charge you a couple of dollars for this or that service. Most times all he does is to put a pre-printed form in an envelope and mail it to you under the heading of 'Strictly Private and Personal'.

Here is another sad little extract from a letter: 'I recently lost a friend of many years, my little pet died and I am broken-hearted and wondering. My parish priest told me that I was a bad woman to dare to suggest that animals have souls, he said that only humans have souls, and more or less implied that only those humans who belong to his own branch of the Church. Can you give me any hope that I will see my beloved pet in another life?'

Some priests are real jackasses, you know. They are astonishingly ignorant men. It always amazes me—well, let us take Christians—Christians almost go to war as to which sect is the true sect, Christians preaching Christianity do not show Christianity to Christians of another sect. Look at the Protestants and the Catholics, you would think they had bought up all the front row seats in Heaven the way they go on. Catholics seem to think that Protestants are evil people, and Protestants are quite sure that Catholics are evil people. But that's not a matter of discussion at present.

For centuries asinine preachers have taught that Man is the ultimate in development, they have taught that there cannot be anything higher than mankind, and mankind alone has a soul provided that they be of this or that specific religion!

I say to you with absolute knowledge that, yes, animals also go to the astral world, animals have the same opportunities as humans. I say to you, yes, you can meet beloved pets again, not merely when you yourself die to this Earth, but now in astral travel to the zone in which those animals are.

Only an utter fool, only a complete and absolute ignoramus such as a priest of some derelict, decadent religion would believe that Man has a sole copyright, so to speak, on souls. Consider this; U.F.O.s are real, there are other people in space, people so highly evolved, so highly intelligent, that intelligent humans now are by comparison to these space people as stupid as a dress shop dummy, you know, one of those plaster or plastic figures standing stiffly in the dress with some hideous frock stuck on over it.

One of the reasons why religious bodies deny the existence of U.F.O.s is because their very presence shows that Man is not the ultimate form of evolution. If the priests are right and Man is the ultimate form of evolution, then what are these people in space? They are real people, they are intelligent people, and some of them are spiritual people. They have souls, they too go to the astral worlds just as do humans, just as do animals, cats, horses, dogs, etc.

Very definitely, very emphatically, and speaking with the utter knowledge of one who does astral travel as a matter of course, let me tell you this; yes, my friend, your pet lives in another sphere, lives in good health and in better shape, even more pleasant to look at, perhaps even missing you, but now with the knowledge that you can meet again, for, as in the case of humans, if you really love your pet and your pet really loves you, you can and you will meet again.

Let me tell you that Mrs. Fifi Greywhiskers, my truly beloved friend, left this Earth some time ago; she is still my beloved friend and I can visit her in the astral. And Miss Ku'ei also left this world when she was badly upset by another attack of press persecution. Miss Ku'ei was ill at the time and these moronic press people thundering around upset her, and—well —she left me. I was sad, sad for myself, sad that I could no longer cradle her in my arms, but glad that she had relief from the sorrows and utter miseries which she and I had endured together on this Earth. I tell you, I meet her in the astral, so I am in a very, very definite position to tell you that the priests are wrong, mankind is not the epitome of spiritual development. Some animals are far more spiritual than Man!

Let us close this chapter, then, with a repetition of that statement. I repeat, yes, all you who grieve for those little pets who have left this Earth and gone on beyond, grieve no more, for if you love your departed pet and that pet loves you, you will be together again beyond the confines of this Earth just as Mrs. Fifi Greywhiskers and the Lady Ku'ei and I meet so often in the astral, and as we shall be together on a much more permanent basis when—may it be soon—this life on Earth ends for me, and when there is a cessation of press persecution and hostility, when there is a cessation of pain and misery which long drawn out illness causes.

CHAPTER TWO

THE old man shifted wearily in the uncomfortable wheelchair. 'No springs,' he muttered, 'even a baby carriage has springs, yet the ones who are sick have to jog along as comfortlessly as in a farm cart!'

It had been a cheerless day, and one which was far from ended. Letters, and MORE letters. All of them WANTING 'You are my father and my mother,' said the letter from Africa, 'and I love you like my best girl friend. Now I want to come and tell you so. Will you send me a free return ticket so that I may? And at the same time send the fare so that I can see my sister who lives in Los Angeles. I shall expect this by return and will kiss the dust at your feet.' The old man sighed ruefully and set the letter aside. 'Thinks I'm a millionaire, does he?' he asked the Little Girl Cat purring alongside.

Old Maggie was out of the mental hospital again and had resumed her barrage of unwanted love letters. Old Maggie! The woman who journeyed to this Canadian seaport and told people she was employed by the old man! Said she was employed by him—ran up a bill for a hundred and sixty-eight dollars in his name and sent a frightened hotel manager to the old man for the money. Money which was not forthcoming. 'I have never even SEEN the woman,' said the old man, 'and she deluges me with letters which I tear up. No, I have no work—or money—for her.' So Old Maggie cheerfully admitted that she had just left a mental home, and she was deported back to one.

Mrs. Horsehed's letter, too, was a bother. Twenty-two pages of it. All questions. Questions which would need a book to answer, THIS book, Mrs. Horsehed. Dear, dear! Mrs. Horsehed, the lady who had things written to her in words of one syllable and who STILL managed to read the wrong meaning in everything!

Yes, the old man was weary. The day was long and the letters were longer. Outside the summer weather of deep, deep fog swirled blackly, smearing windows with a greasy scum, and hiding the ramshackle buildings near the waterfront. Somewhere out in the fog a ship hooted mournfully, as if in despair at having to enter this moribund seaport where the water stank to high heaven with the discharging effluvia of a nearby pulp mill. The old man grunted 'PFAH, what a stench!' and turned to signing the letters—all forty-three of them.

The Little Girl Cat stood up, arched her back and said 'Arrh!' before going off to her tea. The Littlest Girl Cat was still abed recovering from a chill easily induced by the damp fog and intense humidity of these summer days. The wheelchair groaned in dismay beneath the two hundred and sixty pounds of weight as the old man turned to switch on the lights. 'Lights,' he muttered, 'lights, are they really necessary at five in the afternoon of a midsummer's day?'

The years bore down heavily, years of suffering, years of sorrow, years made even more sorrowful by the cowardly men of the press who always printed lies—being strangers to the Truth—and who never dared afford an opportunity for a reply to their columns. Cowardly men, despicable men, who live by pandering to their readers' worst emotions, who drag down culture instead of helping it up.

The dreary evening slowly wore on. The faintest of faint glows showed that somewhere outside the fog-enshrouded windows street lamps were alight. Eerie crawling glimmers, like fireflies afar, showed that late workers were making their slow way home behind straining headlights.

At last it was late enough to retire. The old man trundled his wheelchair to the side of the hard, hard bed and climbed in. With a sigh of relief he settled back. 'Now for freedom,' he thought, 'freedom to wander at will throughout the world by astral travel.' For some moments he rested, lost in thought, then, the night's journey decided upon, he relaxed for the preparatory stages.

Soon there came the familiar slight jerk, almost a start as if one had been frightened, and with the slight jerk the astral body shook free from the physical. Shook free and drifted upwards, higher and higher.

The fog was all around the harbour. A few miles further out the fog thinned and was gone. At the airport the lights were on and the infrequent aircraft were still able to make their landings. Out in the Bay of Fundy a large oil tanker rode at its moorings, rode at anchor, its riding lights swaying slightly as the ship heaved to the change of the tide. Aboard the oil ship men were still playing, gambling with packs of cards before them, and piles of money on the floor. They seemed happy enough, although impatient to get ashore to whatever entertainment this poor port could offer them. Entertainment? What sort of entertainment does the average sailor want? And that can be found in even the poorest of ports, and the poorer the port the cheaper that form of entertainment, although possibly the dearest in the end!

The old man, not old any longer now that he was not encumbered by an ailing body and a creaking wheelchair, drifted along across the Bay of Fundy. He stopped awhile at the little town of Digby nestling between hills, a quaint little place, one which it would be nice to visit in the flesh because in the astral colours are rather different. It's like taking off smoked glasses and seeing things as they are.

From Digby, on to Yarmouth to look at that little place with its narrow streets and crowded houses. Seemed to be just one main street with a few scattered houses around. And—oh yes!—a shockingly crazy woman lived down there!

Move on, move on to Halifax. A slight pause, and the ground blurred beneath, blurred with the speed of travel. And then the lights of Halifax came swiftly into view. Halifax! What an unfriendly city, what a horrible city, was the personal opinion of the old man floating above. He thought for a moment of that stupid old biddy at the airport who said she was a good Catholic, and they didn't want heathens in clean Halifax. Still, that's in days gone by. Today is today, and tomorrow—well, a few miles further on and we shall be in tomorrow. So a circle around Halifax, passing the big Paragon buildings, passing over the Naval Station and the Bedford Basin, seeing the lights atwinkle on the wooded slopes flanking Bedford Basin. The lights of the rich people, the ones who could just buy and order what they like, the ones who could get medical attention and not count the cost. Not like the old man who, because he was so sick, couldn't get insured with the Blue Cross or the Green Shield, or whatever it is. They all seemed to want their cake and eat somebody else's. So the old man could not afford medical attention in young, bustling Canada, and so he suffered because of lack of money, because of lack of medical attention which he could not afford.

So thinking he rose higher and higher, rose up to where he could see the sunlight and sped on across the Atlantic. Soon a satellite came hurtling by, a satellite reflecting bright silver as it caught the rays of the sun. But the old man wasn't bothered by satellites, or anything of that nature. They were too common, too usual.

He sped on and overtook an Air Canada plane shrieking its way across the Atlantic bound for—where? Shannon? Prestwick? Or possibly going straight to Le Bourget in France. Astral travel has many advantages. The plane was overtaken, and passed with no more than a glance in the cabin windows where all the tourist and economy passengers were sitting, three abreast, on both sides of the aisle, with a blue light which simulated night shining dimly down upon them. Some were there with their mouths wide open. And there along the other aisle was a woman with her mouth wide open and her skirts up round her thighs, sound asleep she was, oblivious of the interested gaze of the young man beside her who was wishing that there was more light.

In the pilot's cabin the Captain at the controls was smoking his pipe and looking like a placid old cow seen in an Irish field. His co-pilot, sitting beside him, was looking bored to tears. And the flight engineer, behind them and to the right, was holding his head in his hands as if life was just too too insupportable.

On sped the old man, far outstripping the speed of the plane, the plane which was lumbering behind at perhaps six or seven hundred miles an hour. And soon, over the curve of the horizon, came the loom of the lights of London and the flashing beacon which was London Airport.

Here, in London, the streets were by no means deserted although it was about two o'clock in the morning, a fine morning too. Busy work gangs were moving about sweeping the streets, clearing up the litter, and here and there manholes in the streets were opened and little frames with red flags above them prevented the unwary from falling down. Here were the sewer men carring out their nightly inspection. Deep underground while the rest of London slept.

But how London has changed, the old man thought. This great building stretching up and up! But then he remembered. Oh, yes, of course, that is the new Post Office Tower, supposed to be the highest in England. Thoughtfully, interestedly, he circled around it and saw the men inside more or less killing time. Things weren't very busy at this hour of the night. And then the old man moved on, on through Victoria Street.

A train was just coming into the station and weary passengers were picking up their luggage, and stretching cramped legs. In the taxi ranks the cab drivers were waking themselves up from a light doze, starting their cabs, and waiting for the fares.

But the old man drifted along, looking at familiar places in Victoria Street, and then he spied an immense new building, the windows of which overlooked the gardens of Buckingham Palace. 'What bad taste,' he thought, 'what bad taste! That these building promotors should intrude upon the privacy of the Royal Family who have done so much for England, even against the active opposition of the press who always take any opportunity, no matter how unjustified, of picking faults with the Royal Family. A family who has done more for England than any other Englishman or woman.'

But down below red double-decker buses still roar through the streets carrying night workers to or from their nightly shifts. Perhaps this little jaunt to England should come to an end now, there is so much else to see. But, before leaving England, let us look along the length of Fleet Street again and read some of the early morning headlines. Here it says that the press of England are having a very bad time financially, they cannot put up the price of their papers for people will not pay any more. Sixpence for a newspaper! A lot of money for paper into which one wraps one's fish and chips! 'Personally,' the old man thought, 'the daily newspapers, the whole bunch of them together, they're not worth a halfpenny. And the sooner they go bankrupt the better for the world, for they generate hate between nations and between peoples. Can anyone truly say the press have ever done any good?'

So thinking the old man turned his thoughts southwards, and in the astral flight took a wide sweep straight over the English Channel. Straight over Paris, he went, where he just gave a passing glance at the home of de Gaulle the troublemaker before speeding on to South America, to the River Plate, to the land of Uruguay, Montevideo.

Here in Montevideo the time was about midnight. The streets were still thronged. Demonstrations were in progress. Students were rioting, and even as the old man watched from a few feet above the city a lusty student hand propelled a large rock straight through the face of a clock standing on the sidewalk by a familiar bus stop. There was a shattering of glass and a PFHUT! And a shower of sparks, and the face of the clock grew dark, no longer did it indicate the hours, the minutes, and the seconds.

Around the street corner a gang of grey-uniformed police swirled, sticks in their hands, caps awry, arms outflung to catch any student who came within their reach. The old man floated along thinking of what could have been the future of Uruguay. It could have been a wonderful place. It could have been the Garden of South America, supplying exotic fruits to the rest of the world. It could have been the Switzerland of South America, looking after the money and the financial interests of the whole of North, Central, and South America. But the Uruguayans were unequal to the tasks before them like a man who has never had an illness before and so, not immunised, falls prey to the first slight sickness. Uruguay, with never a bit of suffering, went to pieces when the first storms ruffled their apparently calm surface.

The old man thought of a year or so before when he had visited the astral world, and consulted the Akashic Record of the probabilities and saw what should have been for Uruguay. The interior of Uruguay is arid because the Uruguayans had cut down all the trees, and the land in the interior is almost barren, almost desert, without water, without vegetation, and seems to be only sunbaked earth which, drying and powdering, blows away at the first puff of wind. The Akashic Record of Probabilities showed that the Uruguayans should have floated a loan in neighbouring countries, and should, by carefully controlled atomic blasts, have excavated a great basin perhaps thirty miles by fifty miles in the centre. It would have filled from deep wells because the water is there, below the surface. It would have filled, and would have been a wonderful lake, or lagoon, bringing life to the Land of Uruguay. Then there would have been trees planted all around the shores of the new lake. And the trees would have brought new atmosphere to a devitalised zone. Soon the land would have flourished, it would have been lush pasture land, rich orchards, and land which would have been the Garden of South America.

The Record of Probabilities showed that there would have been a canal leading from the centre of the country along to Maldonado where there is such very deep water and such a very beautiful curve to the shoreline, that it is indeed a natural harbour. The main harbour should have been there, at Maldonado, because the present harbour at Montevideo is silting up, and the whole of the River Plate is now a shallow stretch of water, dredged constantly in the ever-shifting sands.

But the old man floating above, looking down, thinking of all these things, shook his head with sorrow at the thought that the Uruguayans had not measured up to those things which were probabilities for them and which would have led them so profitably to greatness. The Record of Probabilities showed that in years to come Australia would have been impressed by such a successful scheme, and would have copied the scheme in the dead heart of Australia. Where the furnace-like desert dries up everything. But Australia could be opened up as Uruguay could have been opened up.

The old man had seen enough of Uruguay. And so, with just a farewell wave, he lofted higher and higher and sped with the speed of thought across the face of the world. Across oceans, across lands, to another destination.

'I want you to tell us more about astral travel, how we can do it. You've written about it in *You—Forever!* and in other books, but tell us again. You cannot tell us too much about it, tell us how we can do it.'

So go the letters. So go the demands. 'Tell us about astral travel.'

Actually, astral travel is the simplest of things, so simple that it is surprising that people cannot do it without trying. But we must also remember that walking is simple. Walking is so simple that we can walk in a straight line, or follow a curved path, and we do not have to think about it at all. It comes natural to us. Yet on many occasions a person has been very ill and confined to bed for some months, and the sufferer has then forgotten how to walk. He or she has forgotten how to walk, and has had to be taught all over again.

It is the same with astral travel. Everybody could once do astral travel, but for some strange reason they have forgotten precisely how to do it. How do you teach a person how to walk? How do you teach a person, long encased in an iron lung, to breathe?

How do you teach a person to travel in the astral? Possibly only by recounting the steps and the process. Possibly only by being what some would call repetitious can one induce a person to teach his or herself how to get again into the astral.

Suppose you have a sponge, an ordinary big bath sponge will do, and then you call it the body. Suppose you fill the holes in the sponge with a gas which clings together. That is, it doesn't disperse like most gases do, it hangs together like a cloud. Well, this gas you can call the astral. It is now in the sponge, so you have one entity inside another. The sponge representing the body, and the gas filling the otherwise empty spaces in the sponge and representing the astral body. If you shake the sponge you may dislodge the cloud of gas. In the same way, when your body gives a little jerk under controlled conditions the astral body jumps free.

The best way to prepare for astral travel is to think about it. Think about it very seriously from all aspects, because as you think today so you are tomorrow, and what you think about today you can DO tomorrow. Ask yourself why do you want to do astral travel. Ask yourself honestly. What really is your reason? Is it merely idle curiosity? Is it so that you can spy on others, or do you want to fly through the night and peer into bedrooms? Because if that is your objective you would be better off without astral travel. You must be sure that your motives are right before you do astral travel, or even before you try to do astral travel.

Then having assured yourself that your motives will stand the strictest inspection, prepare the next step. When you go to bed, alone, make sure you are not tired. Make sure that you are fresh enough, that you can stay awake. Everyone can do astral travel, but the majority of untrained people fall asleep in the process which is very annoying indeed! So go to bed before you are tired and rest in any way comfortable in your bed, and then THINK that you are moving out of your body. Let yourself become completely relaxed. Have you a tension in your big toe? Does your ear itch? Have you an ache in the small of your back? Any of these will indicate that you are not truly relaxed. You must be truly relaxed, just as a sleeping cat is relaxed. And having been quite sure that you are relaxed, imagine that 'something' is coming out of your body. Imagine that you are the gas seeping out of the sponge. You might experience a little tingling, you might hear some short, sharp crackles, or you may get 'pins and needles' in the back of your neck. Fine! That means you are coming out. Now be very very sure that you keep still. It is utterly necessary that you do not panic, it is absolutely vital that you do not feel fear because panic or fear will slap you back in the body and give you quite a fright. It will also effectively prevent you from consciously astral travelling for about three months.

Astral travel is normal. It is utterly, utterly safe. No one can take over your body, no one can harm you, all that can happen is this; if you are frightened unpleasant astral entities will smell or see the colour of fright, and will with the greatest of glee try to frighten you more. They cannot hurt you, they cannot hurt you at all, but it does give them great pleasure if they can frighten you so much that you are chased back into your physical body.

There is no secret in astral travel, it just needs confidence. It just needs the firm knowledge that you are going to do astral travel while you are fully awake. And the best way to start about it is to imagine that you are travelling, imagine that you are out of the body. This word 'imagination' is badly misused. Perhaps it would be better to say 'picture'. So, picture yourself leaving your flesh body, picture yourself gradually inching out of your flesh body and floating inches above the recumbent flesh body. Actually picture yourself doing it, actually form the strong thoughts that you are doing it, and sooner or later you will do it. You will find, with the greatest amazement, that you are floating there, looking down upon a padded, whitish-green, flesh body. Probably it will have its mouth open, probably it will be snoring away because when you are out it doesn't matter at all if your flesh body goes to sleep—when you are out. Because if you get out while the body is awake, you will remember the whole experience.

This is what you have to imagine: You are resting completely relaxed on your bed in any position which suits you provided it is comfortable and relaxed. Then you think of yourself, slowly edging out from the flesh covering, from the flesh body, slowly edging out and rising and floating a few inches or a few feet above the flesh body. Do not panic even if you do get a few sways and tilts because YOU CANNOT BE HURT. You cannot be hurt at all, and as you are floating you cannot fall. When you have got to that stage, rest awhile. Just keep still, you don't need to feel panic nor triumph, just rest peaceably for a few moments. And then, if you think you can stand the shock, and depending on what sort of a body you've got, gaze down on the thing you've left. It looks all lopsided, it looks lumpy and heavy, it looks an untidy mess. Well, aren't you glad to get away from it for the time being?

With that thought you should take a look at the world outside. So will yourself to rise, will yourself to float up through the ceiling and through the roof. No! You won't feel anything, you won't get a bump or a scrape or a jar. Just will yourself to float up, and picture yourself so floating.

When you get out through the roof stop when you are about twenty or fifty feet above and look about you. You can stop by thinking that you are stopped.

And you can rise by thinking that you are rising. Look about you, look at your surroundings from a viewpoint that you have never seen before so far as you can remember, get used to being out of the body. Get used to moving around. Try floating around the block. It's easy! You just have to tell yourself where you are going, and you just have to tell yourself how fast you are going, that is, do you want to go along slowly as if blown by the breeze, or do you want to go there instantly?

People write and say they have tried everything they know to do astral travel but, for some reason or other, they did not succeed. A person will write and say, 'I had a strange tickling in the back of my neck. I thought I was being attacked and it frightened me.' Another person writes in to say, 'I seemed to be lying on the bed without the power to move, I seemed to be looking through a long red tunnel with a glimmer of something which I cannot describe at the end.' And yet another person writes, 'Oh, my goodness me! I fell out of my body, and I was so frightened that I fell back in again!'

But these are perfectly ordinary, perfectly normal symptoms. Each of these symptoms can occur when you are getting out consciously for the first time. These are good signs. Signs that you are able to astral travel consciously. Signs that you have your hand on the door, so to speak, and the door is slowly opening. But then you take fright right on the threshold of this wonderful experience, you panic, and back you go into that damp, miserable clay case again.

Only fear can cause you any real difficulty. Everything else can be overcome. But fear—well, if you will not master your fear of the apparently unknown, what can one do for you? You have to make some effort yourself. You can't put some money in a slot machine and get some pre-packaged astral travel kit, you know.

Well, when you get a tickling sensation it means that your astral body is actually freeing itself from the physical body, and for some particular reason the process is causing a tickle which is, after all, some slight form of irritation. It just means that you have not been doing astral travel very often, because with practise the separation of the two bodies becomes easier and easier.

Just by way of digression let me tell you this; I was writing this chapter on astral travel, and I suppose I was thinking about it too intensely or something. And immediately I found myself floating above this building—right outside—and looking down. A member of my household was just coming up the road carrying a load of groceries! I saw her come in and have a mild listen at my door to see if I was working or not, and then undecided she passed on to another room. I looked about and thought, 'Oh, my goodness me! I'm shirking!' And dived back again straight into the body, and carried on working. But it just shows that when one is practised in astral travel it is no more difficult to get out of the body than it is to leave a room by opening a door and stepping out. Actually it's less effort. It is far less effort.

When a person is reclining and then suddenly feels paralysed, that is a perfectly normal sign, there is nothing wrong with it. It just means that the separation of the two bodies is preventing physical body motion, and the so-called paralysis is a misnomer really. It is just a strong physical disinclination to move. One often, at the same time, seems to be peering through a long tube, it might be a red tube, or it might be a black or grey tube. But it doesn't matter what colour it is, it is a good sign, it shows you are getting out.

The biggest thing to fear is fear itself, because all these things are perfectly ordinary. There is nothing at all unusual in them. But if you are going to give way to panic, well, you come straight back into the body with a real 'clunk', and if you come back in misalignment, then you'll have a sick headache for the rest of the day, until you go to sleep again and relocate your astral in the physical.

It sometimes happens that one gets slightly out of the body and then a swaying motion is experienced. That's all right, too. It just means you have not learned how to handle the astral body properly. You can think of it as a person learning to steer a motor-car. You get in the wretched thing and give the wheel a turn, and turn too far. So you turn the other way, and you find you are turning too far that way. So you progress in a sort of S curve until you learn to manage the steering properly. It is precisely the same with the astral. You start emerging from the body and then, when you are a few inches out, you sort of lose your nerve, you do not know how to get it out a foot, two feet, etc. And so you stay there swaying. The only thing to do is to visualise yourself as OUT!

Yes, no doubt much of this appears to be repetition to you. Deliberately it is repetition because you need to get this firmly established that astral travel is quite normal and quite easy, and not at all dangerous. The only thing to fear is of being afraid. And you need only fear being afraid because it puts back your progress. It's like locking on the brakes hard. Once you are in a state of fear you are not in control of yourself, and your body chemistry gets jangled. So—do not be afraid, because there is no cause whatsoever to fear anything in the astral.

It really is a superb, a glorious, experience to just get out of your physical body and float along in the air. You do not have to do long journeys, you can let yourself just drift, perhaps thirty or forty feet above the ground. You will feel a gentle rise from air currents, especially when you pass over trees. Trees give a nice up-draught, a warm sort of friendly up-draught, and if you let yourself float and maintain a constant height over a clump of trees when in the astral, you will find that your vitality improves very greatly. But this astral travel is a pleasure which has to be appreciated. There are no words which can adequately describe it. You are out of the body and you feel free, you feel as if you had been recharged with life. You feel as if you are sparkling all over, and it is one of the best experiences of all. It can be your experience too, you know, if you really want it. Thousands of people have written to me saying how surprisingly easy they now find astral travel, telling me of their travels, and telling me that they have seen me on their astral travels. What these people can do, you can do also.

But let us go into the matter a little further to try to find out what is preventing you from enjoying this wonderful experience.

First of all, do you sleep alone? That is in your own room. Because if you share a bed with someone else then you may find it a bit difficult. There is always the fear that another person turning over will disturb one's astral flight. So, while initiating astral travel, you should always be alone, quite alone in your room. One cannot, for example, easily practise astral travel when one lives in barracks with a lot of other men or a lot of other women. Nor can you easily start astral travel if you have just been married! You have to be alone, you have to keep your mind on astral travel and then you can do it.

From letters it appears that the greatest vice of those who are trying to astral travel is impatience. North Americans in particular want 'instant astral travel'. They are not prepared to wait for it, nor to work for it, they have no patience. They want a thing faster than fast and quicker than now. Well, it's not done in that way, you have to be in the right condition first. You have to exercise patience just as if you had been in bed a long time you would have to exercise patience while you were relearning to walk. Have patience, then, and have faith that you can do this thing. Visualise yourself floating above your body because 'imagination' is a most potent force. And if you can get yourself started, well, the rest is utterly simple. Astral travel is the simplest thing that we can do. Even breathing needs some effort. Astral travel needs the absolute negation of effort.

After impatience the next great fault preventing one from getting into the astral state is over-tiredness. People flap about all day, rushing about like a hen with its head chopped off, dashing to the cinema or to the supermarkets and cavorting around the country. Then, when they are nearly dropping with tiredness, they get in bed and think they will do astral travel. Well, they do, but they are so tired that they go to sleep and forget all the travelling, or rather forget all the experiences of that travel. Make no mistake about it, you do astral travel when you are asleep, the trick is to stay awake and do it, and it is just a knack which one has to acquire as one gets the knack of breathing. The doctor slaps one's bottom when one is born and one draws an outraged breath so that one can yell in protest, and breathing is started. Well, I can't come and slap you all on the bottom to start you astral travelling! But it really is a simple matter and needs just a little knack.

Impatience and over-tiredness, then, are the two great causes of failure to remember. There is another cause—constipation.

If you are constipated you are usually so gloomy that the poor wretched astral form is imprisoned in a congested lump of clay. Constipation is the curse of civilisation, and perhaps as it is so important for our astral travel studies that one be not constipated, we should devote a whole chapter to health things. So— read on later in this book on how to get rid of constipation. When you get garbage out of your body you will find that you are so much freer that you can get into the astral.

Someone wrote to me and said, 'But look. All these astral bodies that you say float around by day and by night, why don't their Silver Cords get entangled, why don't they collide? You say that thousands of people leave their bodies and soar upwards like balloons on the end of a string. How can this be without hopeles tangling occurring?'

The answer to that is easy; everyone has a different frequency, every physical body has a certain frequency and the astral body has a frequency several— well, I'm not musical—but let me say 'octaves' higher. The astral body is obviously on a harmonic of the physical body, but the vibration is many million times faster than in the physical body. Everyone has a different frequency, or different rate of vibration, and if you get the B.B.C., London, on your radio, you get the B.B.C., London. You do not get Radio Turkey or Radio Pekin on that wavelength or frequency.

One could say that the frequencies of radio stations do not interfere with each other, and in the same way the frequencies of different astrals do not interfere with each other so thay cannot collide—so there is no tangling, no confusion. On a busy street in a busy city you will have people bumping into each other, and either apologising or scowling, according to their make-up, but such things never occur in the astral. There are no collisions. The only ones that can come close to each other in the astral worlds above the lower astral are those who are compatible. You cannot have discord, and a collision is usually a discord, is it not?

Everyone knows that many people say, 'This problem—I can't deal with it now, I'll sleep on it. I shall have the answer in the morning.' Well, that's fair enough, because people with problems take the problem into the astral world and if they can't solve it themselves there is always someone available who can. And then if they can't do conscious astral travel, they still come back with some memory of how the problem can be solved. People like great musicians go to the Other Side and go to a zone above the lower astral. They hear this wondrous spiritual music, and then, because they are basically musical, because they have musical perception, they memorise it. And when they awaken in the morning—or they might even waken specially—they rush to a musical instrument and, as they think 'compose'. Some great composers kept paper and pencils by the bedside so that if they woke up with 'inspiration' they could write down the musical notation immediately. This is stuff they have learned in the astral, this is music which they learned in the astral. And it is a legitimate use of astral travel.

A great inventor may have seen something in the astral, but possibly he didn't do astral travel consciously. So when he awakens in the morning he has a wonderful idea for a new 'invention', and he rushes to his notebooks and he writes down specification and draws squiggles. And then—well, he has invented something which the world has wanted for quite a long time.

Many highly successful businessmen use astral travel consciously or unconsciously. This is how it works; a man who is very successful at interviewing decides that he has a very tough person to see on the morrow. So when he is in bed he goes through his routine and he talks to himself, and says what he proposes to say to his 'prospect' when he meets him tomorrow. He anticipates the objections and arguments of the prospect and he refutes them as he lies there in bed. Then he falls asleep. His astral has got the idea and when the physical body is asleep the astral gets out and goes in search of the body, or the astral, of the prospect, and tells the prospect what is going to be said on the morrow and also tells the prospect what action the latter should take.

On the morrow at the interview the two greet each other like old friends, they are sure they have met before. They find they are getting along famously, and the successful interviewer puts over his points to the prospect and really does get the action desired. It is simple, highly successful, and entirely legitimate. So, if you want to get success in business or love—well, go in for astral travel. You get your word in first. You get the action you desire firmly implanted into the prospect's mind.

A lot has been said about getting out of the body, and you can get out of the body. Once out you can always return. I suppose never in history has there been an authentic case when a person could not get back. You can get back all right, but you want to get back in the most pleasant conditions because if you get all slap-happy and just jump into your clay case you can get a headache.

When you are coming back from your astral travel you see your flesh body lying there on the bed, usually in a contorted attitude. Eyes shut, mouth open, limbs in wild abandon perhaps, and you have to get into that body. Visualise yourself lowering, and lowering, and lowering. Oh! So gently! Then when you are just barely out of contact, put your own limbs in precisely the same attitude as that of the physical body. And then let yourself be absorbed into the body like moisture being absorbed by blotting paper. You are in the body (it's a cold and clammy thing indeed) but you are in and there has been no shock, no jerk, no unpleasantness. But supposing you were clumsy and you got in with an awful jerk. Then you'll find that you've got an awful headache, you'll find that you feel sick. There is only one thing to do—no medicine, no drugs, will help you at all—there is only one possible cure and it is this:

You must lie still with your feet together and your hands together, and you must let yourself go to sleep, even though it be for a few moments only—go to sleep so the astral body can ease out of the physical body and then sink down and relocate exactly. When it is relocated exactly you have a sense of wellbeing and no headache. And—that's all there is to it!

In this chapter quite a lot has been said about astral travel, far more than need have been said. But the whole idea was to repeat things from different angles so that you could perhaps grasp the underlying statement that it is so very, very easy. You can do it provided you do not try too hard. You can do it provided you have patience. You cannot go along to a ticket agency or travel agency and just book an astral flight, you know. Some of the flights cost a lot of money, but in the astral world it's all free. And you can have it—for free—if you have patience and are not too tired.

So go to it. It truly is a wonderful, wonderful sensation.

CHAPTER THREE

JOHN THOMAS was a fine, upstanding young member of the little Welsh community. A loyal, vociferous member of the 'Wales for the Welsh—Look you' Movement, he was an acknowledged leader of the group who shouted invective when the Prince of Wales to-be appeared in the Principality. Loud and shrill he was, indeed, when he translated strange bardic oaths into the English language and hurled them at the heads, or ears, of English tourists harmlessly visiting the Seat of Welsh Culture.

Down at the 'Leek and Daffodil' he threw a pretty dart 'at the heart of the English Tyrant, whateffer, look you,' as he stopped for a moment or so from his endless beer imbibing. Many were the tales he told of English atrocities as he waited for his unemployment benefit provided free by a parsimonious England.

By night he would steal out with a paint-pot and brush and, first making sure he was unobserved, paint witty remarks on any convenient wall—always against the English, of course. But one day he appeared at the 'Leek and Daffodil' looking grim and glum as well as morose amd moody. 'What is it that ails you, John Thomas?' enquired a friend. 'You look kind of wilted!'

John Thomas sighed and groaned and wiggled his ears. 'Ah, woe is me!' he exclaimed, rolling his eyes heavenwards but keeping a tight hold of his tankard. 'Woe is me, my dole has run out and I can get no more from the filthy English, now I shall have to work in the Land of my Fathers!' He turned away and quickly grabbed the filled tankard of a man whose attention had been distracted. Draining the stranger's first, then his own, he hastened away.

Next day, with heart-felt lamentations, he took a job as a tourist bus driver and was henceforth known as Thomas the Bus. Sadly, sadly, he drove English tourists on their excursions, answering their questions with a pleasant smile, but holding black murder in his heart. Days wore on and Thomas the Bus wore out. More and more morose he became, look you, and no longer was his voice raised in song. No longer did he raise the tankard for even gift beer. He grew lethargic, listless, languid, and lazy. No longer did he daub graffita on the walls at night, no longer did he object or raise a commotion when, being detected in short-changing his tourists, an Englishman sang,

> 'Taffy was a Welshman,
> Taffy was a thief,
> Taffy came to our house
> And stole a round of beef.'

'It is under the weather that I am indeed,' he quoth to a crony, 'and I feel that my shadow is more substantial than I myself am, perhaps I should hie me forth and consult Old Williams the Med.' Off he tottered on shaking limbs and painfully hauled himself up the three steps to Williams the Med.

Dr. Williams soon disposed of the other patients and called in Thomas the Bus, exclaiming, 'Well, what is it with you, my man?'

'Oh, Dr. Williams,' exclaimed Thomas the Bus, 'I can sing no more and I cannot raise my tankard.' He looked about furtively and then in a conspiratorial whisper mumbled, 'That's not all I can't do either.' His voice sank lower and lower, and at last Dr.

Williams said, 'Yes, my man, I know exactly what is wrong with you. As Thomas the Bus you are crouched over your controls and it has constricted your bowels.' His voice rose to an angry roar, 'You are constipated, my man, CONSTIPATED—full of useless rubbish. Would you have rubbish in your house? Wouldn't you take it outside for the sanitary attendant's attention?'

Thomas the Bus hung his head in shame, and he mumbled, 'Yes, my bus goes every day but I only go once a week.'

I receive many many letters, thirty or forty a day as I have already stated, and a surprising number are about medical problems. Many people, women especially, do not feel very happy about going to see a doctor and discussing some of the more common and perhaps embarrassing illnesses, dysfunctions, or complaints, so they write to me. In this chapter I am going to deal with one or two health problems, but the first one of all is—constipation!

This is probably the most insidious complaint or illness ever to afflict mankind. One takes action about other types of illness. If you have bad toothache you have the wretched thing yanked out. If you have a broken leg you have the bones set. But constipation——! People seem to think it is like the poor, always with us.

Many people place great faith in the wise words of doctors, but doctors are often in the hands of the pharmaceutical manufacturers. The common cold, and even more common constipation, are what one might term the 'bread and butter' illnesses of the pharmacists. Billions of pounds or dollars have been and will be spent on 'cures' for colds and constipation. Well, the doctor abides, or should abide, by two ancient laws, the first of which states that the art of medicine consists of amusing the patient while

Nature cures the illness. The second is '*primum non nocere*' which means 'first do no harm'. Whatever a doctor does, then, should be in accordance with those two laws, the first—gain the patient's interest and hope that Nature will cure the illness, and second—do no harm. Unfortunately, in the opinion of many people the doctor is doing a great harm when he omits to warn people of the dangers of constipation.

Constipation interests us who want to do astral travel for the sole reason that if a person is habitually constipated it is not possible to do conscious astral travel while one is fully awake. So, if you want to go out on astral journeys make sure that your inside is all right first. Inner cleanliness is important, isn't it?

The very ancient Chinese medical records indicate that early Chinese leaders, emperors and empresses, and great warlords, used clysters to make sure that their interior was at least as clean as their exterior. A common name for clysters nowadays is enema, so let us use the common name because clysters rather reminds one of the cloisters in some old church and we are far removed from that when we deal with enemas! The very early Chinese used narrow bamboo tubes fitted into larger tubes, and that had a piston which propelled the herbal solution into the intestines.

The Egyptians as well got into the act, possibly they got the idea from the Chinese. But round about 1500 B.C. the Egyptians were using enemas as an ordinary routine method of treating ill health. The idea was, if you have a pain inside you get rid of all the waste product which probably causes it. Some of their enema solutions were distinctly messy, oil and honey blended together was quite a common matter!

In French times, in about 1400 or so, enemas were very much in use. Soon after that the enema became a fashionable method of treating illness and many very high-ranking families had at least one enema a day.

In England, also, the leading families had wonderful enema syringes manufactured so that the patient sat over a hole in a wooden box and then a very ornate enema syringe was placed in position, and the handle pumped which injected a carefully prepared liquid into the bowels of the sitting patient. After which the patient arose and departed in great haste so that the load could be discharged. But fashions change. It's not now so fashionable to use the enema. One goes instead to the local drug store and gets a packet of this or a packet of that, and either swallows, sucks, chews, or drinks some noxious concoction which all too frequently gives one a bad pain and violent expulsion, and really does nothing to cure the complaint. Does nothing to overcome that which caused the constipation. It seems now that people want to cure the symptom without curing the root cause which, of course, is too crazy for comment.

Yes, medical treatment undergoes cycles of popularity and unpopularity. It used to be that people had their tonsils removed as a fashionable thing. Then it became the fashion to have the appendix removed, and now it is the fashion for women to have hysterectomy—of which, more later.

But it was a very bad change in fashion when enemas were discontinued because a correctly applied enema can do wonders in overcoming constipation, not merely the system but the lack of health which causes the constipation in the first case. Many people are constipated because they do not drink nearly enough water. One really must drink loads and loads of water if one is to be healthy, because we eat food and it gets churned into a paste inside and then as it passes through the intestines nutritious substances are extracted from the paste and, inevitably, moisture also is extracted. So by the time all the unwanted residue from the food gets into the descending colon it becomes a hard, dry mass. It is expelled by spasmodic screwing-like motions of the colon, and if the mass is too hard then it cannot be expelled, or if it is expelled it causes pain and irritation. The only way to make this mass easily removed is to be sure that there is adequate moisture in it so that it remains as a pliable paste. Too many of the commercial laxatives on the market today are irritants, that is the action of the chemical in the laxative irritates the bowel and makes it twitch. Sometimes it irritates the bowel so much that moisture is drawn from the blood stream through the wall of the colon and saturates the mass of residue. And that causes dehydration!

Many of you have written to me about this very problem, and so the best thing to do is to treat first the original condition by means of a self-administered enema and then, when that condition has been restored to normal, by a very carefully selected laxative when needed. Perhaps, to save another avalanche of letters about this problem, we should go into some more detail. So here it is.

People nowadays eat artificial food, manufactured food, and frequently it lacks bulk. If a person takes food and there is not enough residue to fill the intestine, the motion of the intestine cannot push forward the residue which we desire to excrete. So it is quite essential to have a suitable diet. The diet must include bulk, bulk enough to fill the intestine to its normal size so that the spasmodic twitching of the intestine can move forward that residue. Then the food should have 'roughage', which stimulates the bowel without irritating it, in much the same way as suitably applied massage can stimulate the body without irritating it.

Further, one must drink a lot of water so that there is an adequate water supply to keep the blood at its correct thickness (or density), and enough water to keep the kidneys active, and enough left over to keep the body waste in suitably moist condition. If one follows a normal, sensible diet, plenty of fruit and plenty of vegetables, the bowels should not trouble one unduly. But too many people perch on drug-store stools like a lot of broody hens while they crouch over a plate and absolutely shovel food into their mouth, ladling it in as quickly as possible, hardly taking a bite but swallowing as fast as they can. All this mess gets inside the stomach, and the poor old stomach has to work even harder breaking up the stuff.

Then after one has had this meal one rushes out to catch a bus or do shopping during the lunch-hour break. The bowels during the day get tired of informing their owner that they want to get working, and so the impulse gets slower and slower and weaker and weaker. Many people do not devote enough time to the calls of Nature, and people like bus drivers, for example, who are crouched up in the driver's cabin, constrict their intestines and so constipation is almost an occupational hazard of bus drivers. People seem to think that bowels should only work when THEY want them to work, and they also think that there should be 'instant delivery'.

Nature doesn't work that way. You have to give Nature time to work properly and if you abuse Nature, if you abuse your natural functions, you are going to pay for it with bad health, a bad temper, and a bad bank account.

Now, you know what an enema is? You can get from a drug store a suitable rubber bag with a length of tubing that has a nozzle at the end. With any decent enema bag there will be instructions for use, and it is very very seriously suggested that you shall use an enema for a few times to get your health in good condition because when your intestines have been reconditioned, then you should not again suffer from constipation unless you have some grave disease, in which case you should be in the care of your doctor. Please remember that I am not trying to replace your family doctor. I am not prescribing what one might term medical treatment. I am, instead, trying to save you a lot of misery by telling you some elementary facts which everyone should know, and which, if people would listen, would save them years of illness and much expense with a doctor who really has more important cases to attend to. So, will you remember that. I am not prescribing medical attention for people with serious illnesses, I am suggesting a treatment, a routine which will help you to keep good health. And that means—avoiding constipation.

It is always safe to give an enema, and the best position is when the patient lies perhaps on a towel on the bathroom floor. Lie on the left side with your knees drawn up. You can administer the enema yourself without any difficulty. If you have some really bad constipation trouble it is a very good idea to have a half ounce of tincture of myrrh and about fifteen drops of tincture of echinacea. These should be added to a quart of water which is at approximately body temperature. Put this in your enema bag and inject it into the bowels. Keep it in as long as you can, and the mixture will saturate the hard mass within the bowels and make it soft so that it may be passed without any pain.

After you have expelled the first lot, have another enema injection, but this time with a quart of body temperature water to which only fifteen drops of echinacea has been added. That means you do not have the tincture of myrrh with the second enema. This second injection will help you get rid of any pus or catarrh which is lodged within your lower bowel.

You may be interested to know that many patients who cannot take food through the mouth and throat can be fed 'per rectum'. A nourishing liquid food is very slowly injected and retained, and that nourishes the body. Remember, the more quickly you inject any solution into the rectum, the more quickly it is expelled. And if you want to retain a healing liquid for some time, then the enema should be given very slowly. Naturally you will only inject liquid food under orders of your doctor.

Native tribes throughout the world have their own cures for constipation. The natives of South America, specifically in the interior of Brazil, gave us one of our most famous laxatives—cascara, or, as it is correctly termed, cascara sagrada, the sacred bark. Natives of Brazil go to their witch doctor when they are constipated and get a piece of the sacred bark which they then chew—and a ghastly taste it has, too! After they have chewed for a bit they discreetly retire into some dense bushes and are not seen again for some little time. When they do appear they are much better in health, but possibly a little pale from all the events which have happened. Sacred bark just chewed has a most devastating effect, but now it has been tamed by chemists, and it can be obtained in very suitable graded doses.

When you have got your interior freed from clogging waste you should check your diet and alter it as and when necessary, and you should then ensure regularity of bowel movements by eating properly and by making a habit of attending to the calls of Nature. Go at the same time each day, never mind if for a day you cannot get any result, still sit there and think about it. If you make an absolute habit of it and show Nature that you are there ready and willing, Nature will oblige if you are 'there ready and willing'.

The best laxatives that you can take are the herbal ones. You can get cascara sagrada in tablets or in liquid, and you can get senna in tablets or in liquid. These will produce the desired action without pain. Some of the other chemical concoctions on the market are really dreadfully dangerous, but one could call cascara 'faith pills'. And you will remember that 'faith' moves mountains.

Oh, yes, and do not forget this; it is useless to take a laxative unless you drink enough water. What is the use of taking a laxative which can cause bowel movements when the stuff you want to move is too hard to be moved? It is an utter essential that when you take a laxative you drink a lot of water, otherwise the laxative will just cause pain without producing any good result. Remember, you cannot drink too much water. If you try to drink too much—well, you just find that you can't.

So, your health depends very largely upon having a clean interior. If you have a clean interior then you can get on and do astral travelling.

Another thing which I have been asked to write about by many women is the change of life, the menopause. Many women fear this worse than death, they think they will go insane or something. They have listened to truly fantastic tales and they fear the worst without knowing anything about it. The menopause is a time of change, but you had a change when you became adolescent. A woman doesn't become a child-bearer overnight; what happens is that a girl child ambles along in childish ways until she is—well, it varies with the individual, twelve, thirteen, fourteen years of age—and all the time she is aware of strange things happening inside her. Her attitude to life changes. Her body changes, too, because at a certain time of her life various new chemicals are being manufactured by the body and released into the bloodstream. The girl then finds she has her first period, and after she has had her first period she is capable of bearing a child.

But this changing from childhood to adolescent means that all sorts of chemicals are pouring into her blood, preparing her for motherhood, making her one of the possible child-bearers. But then, at a certain time in her life, the supply of chemicals gradually dies out or dries up and the woman all too often feels that she is now useless, feels that she cannot have a child any longer so everything will be different. She feels that she won't have any sex life. It's crazy, of course. Many people have the happiest time of their life when they have entered the menopause. Many people find they become great artists or great designers or great musicians after the child-bearing age is over. Nature takes away the child-bearing potentialities, but all the energy, all the initiative, everything, can then go into other things. Art, being a good wife, etc. Because when a wife is bothered with small children then she is not necessarily a good wife to her husband. After the menopause she can be, and women can have the happiest time of their life after the menopause.

Women ask me how they should behave at the menopause. The answer is, remember you are undergoing change, you are like a car which for years has been running on petrol and suddenly it has to run on paraffin. With adjustment it can be done quite satisfactorily. Remember that the menopause is utterly natural, every woman gets it, and the only ones who are badly affected are those who worry too much. There is no need to bother about it. Realise that changes are taking place. Realise that if you keep calm about it the changes will be effected more quickly. You may have rather more headaches than average, average for you that is, when the menopause is taking place, but that will pass. Soon things will level out and you won't get any feeling of strangeness any more. You won't get any monthly disturbances any more either, you'll be happier. Many people put on a little weight after the menopause because the various chemicals which have now been stopped made a person quite attractive and burned up excess fat. With the stoppage of those chemicals a body can get a little plump, but with suitable dieting, suitable exercise, you can control that, and look even better. Do not under any circumstances believe Old Wives' Tales, who tell you that you'll get as fat as a pig, you'll enter a mental home, you'll have a beard and a moustache, and all that rubbish.

The menopause is natural, it's quite ordinary, but if you do get too upset or disturbed your doctor can prescribe suitable hormone treatment for you. Now, you cannot prescribe hormones for yourself because there are many different types of hormones and if you take the wrong type they will not do you a bit of good. If you find life too insupportable during the menopause stage, see your doctor, tell him straight out that you want something done about it. Many doctors, sad to say, think that the menopause is so ordinary that it's just a waste of time, it's just childishness for a woman to complain, and if your doctor is like that, then you tell him straight out what you want and see you get it. And if he won't give you hormone treatment, go to some doctor who will because doctors are two a penny, you know.

While we are on the subject of women's complaints, let us refer to that operation known as hysterectomy. Now many women are having hysterectomy without knowing what it's all about. Hysterectomy is almost a status symbol with some women just the same as wearing these comic plastic helmets is a status symbol in Canada or the U.S.A. Men who want to be known as rugged he-men wear a silly little plastic helmet of varying colours to denote their grade —such as building, scaffolding, digging ditches, or gardening (yes, even gardeners wear funny little helmets over here!)

So women, then, are using hysterectomy as a status symbol. It's the newest form of thing just as people had their tonsils out, then they had their appendix out, now they are having their ovaries out. Many women, married women—yes, the unmarried ones as well!—will not bother about birth control, instead they have hysterectomy, which is the removal of the womb and ovaries, and then they just can't have any babies any more. So they can have as much sex as they want, and everything is quite safe.

It's not as easy as all that. Hysterectomy is a very bad thing indeed unless one has a very definite disease. If your doctor tells you that you have a disease and you need hysterectomy do not just take his word for it, go and see another doctor and get his opinion. Regrettably, it's an easy matter to tell a woman to have an operation. It doesn't hurt the doctor and it brings in some money, you know, and doctors are becoming more and more businessmen. They have to live, they have to pay for expensive cars and establishments, and if a woman is willing to pay for an operation—well, it doesn't hurt the doctor. You will understand that I have no faith in these Western doctors. Having had some experience of them in Canada I think they are nothing but glorified butchers. But back to our hysterectomy.

If it is quite essential for you to have the operation, remember that it is in effect an artificial menopause, an artificial change of life. You are not a useless cabbage after it. You can lead a perfectly normal life, and the only difference in your outlook is that you cannot have babies any more. It is very very wrong, though, for a young woman of, let us say, twenty-five to thirty, to have hysterectomy as a form of birth control, because a woman of forty or fifty has lived a normal sex life and her body and Overself have become matured accordingly. But if before any maturing occurs the drastic operation of hysterectomy takes place, then the woman doesn't have any of these experiences which come with periods, etc., etc. If Nature wanted women to have a change of life at twenty-five years of age, Nature would have arranged it accordingly, and it is not right for Man to alter

Nature just for stupid, idle, whims, but only when there is gross disease which cannot be cured by other means.

So, ladies, if you have to have hysterectomy, act as if you had had a serious operation and a change of life at the same time because that's what it is. Remember that with a normal, natural change of life the cessation of flow of various chemicals has taken place over quite a length of time, but if you have had hysterectomy then you get a quite drastic cessation of flow and a difference of chemical output. That is why some women get a bit 'peculiar' when they have had hysterectomy. Because everything has been too drastic and they did not know what to expect. What to expect is this: you have to recover from the physical shock of the operation, and you have to get used to a difference in your chemical composition. You have to realise that for a time you will feel disorientated, lost, unsure of yourself. You may be trembly, you may have headaches, you may have vague pains in the lower part of your body. But, if you will let them, they will pass and you can do normal things again. You can enjoy sex, you can enjoy sports.

But it all depends upon YOUR attitude, upon YOUR frame of mind, because as you think so you are.

One of the big causes of hysterectomy, frigidity, etc., in women—well, a man wouldn't have hysterectomy, now, would he?!—is that parents of the 'old school' often told their children horrible things about sex. Mothers a few years ago taught their daughters that sex was terrible, horrible, despicable, disgusting, and just about everything in that line with a result that they preconditioned the daughter to abhor sex, preconditioned the daughter to be the one responsible for failure in marriage.

I know a woman who was so utterly terrified about sex by her mother that, although she is now in name a married woman, she knows nothing about her husband's body and he knows the same about her. He is a good natured fellow without any drive, without any ambition, as one would expect from the foregoing, and these people live a life as exciting as a lettuce and a cabbage living together in the same shelf of the freezer. I mentioned sex once to this woman, and she nearly threw a fit with embarrassment, horror, and shock, and in my considered opinion she is just about insane because of the fear of sex. She is always afraid of being raped.

It is a tragic thing that mothers shall give daughters such a wholly false idea about sex. But not only mothers are to blame. Many people who claim to be occultists tell others that sex is unclean, sex stops one from progressing in occult studies. Nothing can be further from the truth. There are certain people who need sex, and there are others who do not. You cannot class humans all in one bunch, what suits one group does not suit the other. And I state quite definitely that there is no harm in sex, but only good, provided the practitioners of the art are in love with each other. If they are not in love then the sex act is nothing but elimination the same as other eliminations of the body.

Unfortunately certain Churches, notably the Catholic Church, teach a lot of rot about sex. So far as I have been able to determine the Catholic Church was started by a lot of old men who were scared stiff of women, but they were not so scared of other men and small boys! That may shock some, but if any of you are shocked then get down to a bit of study and find out for yourself. If you have some money go along to the Vatican, and if you can think of a good enough story you will be able to see some of the books, history books, in the Libraries. And in connection with this it amuses me immensely to know that in the Vatican there is the biggest collection of erotica, or pornographic pictures, of anywhere in the Western world.

And yet the Catholics preach against sex.

Sex is normal, sex is natural, sex is utterly necessary to some people, and anyhow what right has a Catholic priest to dictate to other people? How can a Catholic priest, an unmarried man, tell a married woman what she should or should not do? He's talking about things of which he knows nothing—or should know nothing if he truly is a Catholic priest.

Perhaps we should start a campaign against breathing, let us tell some of these Catholic priests that they commit a mortal sin every time they draw a breath, or every time they attend to the calls of Nature. By the look of some of them they don't commit many mortal sins, do they? You'll gather from this that I do not like Catholic priests, and that is perfectly correct, I think they are a bigoted lot. Instead of research to find anything out about the Bible, to find out anything about the Founder of Christianity, they just swallow the Bible lock, stock, and barrel. Take that old tale about Adam and Eve, the Serpent and the apple; well, according to Eastern Teachings the Serpent becomes the male organ, and the apple is the container which holds the seed. And if you read some of the Bible in the light of Eastern knowledge you will agree that there is quite a lot in the Eastern way of thinking.

Moses was found in the bulrushes; sure he was found in the bulrushes. But he was placed there by the Gardeners of the Earth, that is the people who are known as U.F.O. people, to be found. And later in life Moses ascended into the Mountain, Moses did a lot of strange things. But if you re-read the relevant chapters you will find that Moses stepped upon a terraced floor; did he do that on a mountain, or did he step into a flying ship, a U.F.O.? Moses had a Rod of Power; it wasn't made on Earth, you know, it was made on another world. Moses was, in fact, another spaceman specially planted on Earth.

We will deal more with that type of thing in the next chapter, but I want to put on record that for sheer bigotry and ignorance the Roman Catholic priest is hard to beat. I know, I've met loads of them. And I don't like any of them! I have tried to discuss religion with them sensibly and with an honest desire for knowledge, but the Catholic priest always loses his temper, fiddles with his collar, turns red, and bolts. So much for Catholic priests!

Now, I get frequent letters from people who are interested in drugs like LSD, marijuana, peyote, and all the rest of the junk. A surprising number of such people write to me from prisons throughout the U.S.A. They ask me what I think of LSD, what I think of marijuana, and all the rest of it, and it might be interesting to put my definite opinion down here:

LSD, marijuana, peyote, and all these drugs are terribly, terribly harmful to the Overself. If you want to injure yourself—well, that's your own choice, but it is not a good thing to injure your Overself because down here you are only one tenth conscious, so you don't KNOW what the other nine tenths want. Drugs of this type tangle the Silver Cord, make depressions and twists in the aura, and leave harmful scars on the astral body. There is no sense whatever in injuring your body just in search of fresh sensations which are false sensations, anyhow. The only use for any of these drugs is in the hands of qualified medical researchers who can be assumed to know what they are doing or they wouldn't be qualified medical researchers.

My advice is—and this advice never varies—stay away from drugs. If you have to have medical attention requiring drugs, see your doctor. But don't meddle with drugs yourself, you will be doing more harm than you can imagine possible. So—that brings us on to another subject.

Many people seem to think that they are committing a crime if they have any illness. I had a letter from a lady who was of the opinion that she could not make any spiritual progress, any occult progress, because she had a physical infirmity. She was most distressed thinking that she had sinned greatly in having a body that was not perfect.

Do you know, the really healthy person just cannot do any occult work at all! Look at some of the football players, the baseball players, and all those people, just look at a photograph of them. They might be lumps of meat, but too many of them seem to be lacking in the top storey. Just look at those photographs of popular players, and express your own opinion!

Quite seriously, though, I tell you that so far as I am aware one has to have some infirmity before one can be really psychic. The Great Oracle of Tibet was a sick man, a very sick man indeed, and a very accurate one in his prophecies. If you dig down in research you will find that all occultists who are genuine have some physical disability which increases their rate of vibration up to a point where they are able to perceive, either by clairvoyance or telepathy or some other way. That's something for you to think about. Many times a person has an infirmity or illness, not because he or she is working out kharma but so that he or she can have the personal vibration increased to such an extent that higher frequencies may be received, and occult phenomena may be experienced.

People write to me and say that I must have a terrible kharma to work out because I have had coronary thrombosis, T.B., and a few other complaints, and because I have truly had such a terribly hard life. But—no, no it's not working out kharma at all, it is for the purpose of doing a special task. So please do not write again telling me I must have been very wicked in a past life or I would not have suffered so much in this! I know what I was in a past life, I know what I am doing, and I know where I am going.

And I would get there a lot faster if there were more people to help. I have tried to do a special research in the matter of the human aura, I have tried to produce a special device so that anyone can see the aura, but always there is the question of money. If one tries to get money for research—then one is automatically suspect. I have tried to get people to study, but there again people are scared stiff of being parted from anything between their shoes and their hat.

But I do assure you—no! I am not working out kharma. Instead I am doing a special task.

It is unfortunate that so much about human bodies enters into that task because always there is the thought in peoples' minds, 'Oh! He wants money! Oh, he wants sex!' Well, in the latter they are quite wrong! But it does give me an opportunity of saying that the so-called promiscuous Norwegians, or Scandinavians, are quite right in their attitude towards sex, quite right in their attitude towards the human body. After all, Christians claim that the human body is made in the image of God, and then they go and spoil everything by being afraid to show the image of God. The Scandinavians are not like that, they are more broadminded, as are quite a number of Europeans and, of course, the Japanese. But American people, or rather North American people, are really frightfully immature when it comes to human bodies and sex. They don't know what love is, all they want to do is sit in a convertible under the light of the moon and NECK. They want to poke and prod and squeeze, and stir up all the emotions while denying Nature the last emotion of all. And in doing this 'necking' stunt, they build up frustration, misunderstanding, and unhappiness. However, North America is a young continent yet, and I look upon them as toddlers experimenting with themselves and with others, and just starting the long process of growing up.

In ordinary sex, for instance, even with a married couple who may be staying with their parents, they are afraid to make love in case the parents will hear! Well, good gracious me, if the parents hadn't done the same thing sometime before there wouldn't be this married couple now, would there? Which brings us back to what I said before. There is nothing wrong in sex, provided it is done with love. And the people who preach against sex are preaching against the strongest thing in human life, and in my opinion they are just crackpots.

I have just received a letter which asks me about people who are dying. 'Is it true,' the letter asks, 'that people often smile when they are dying?' Yes, they do. Anyone who has had much to do with the very ill and the dying can testify to this; most people when they are at the point of death smile and look happy. They look, in fact, as if they are just being met by loved ones—which is indeed the case! When your time comes to leave this Earth, then, be of good cheer, for you will be met, you will be helped, and there is nothing whatever to fear. On the Other Side of this life, at the Other Side of the curtain we call 'death', there is happiness, light, and joy. But wait for it—wait for it. You cannot die before your time, and if you try to you will get slapped back here in worse conditions. It's worth waiting for, though, it is a very pleasant experience as soon as you have left this Earth.

I have said quite a lot about doctors, said they are two a penny. Yes! The average sort of doctor nowadays is just a businessman, he is out to get a living, he is out to make as much money as he can. So if you consider you have some illness which needs treatment you should search around a bit and find a good doctor, find the best general practitioner you can. The 'general practitioner' differs from the specialist in that the former can diagnose and treat almost any type of illness. You will hear reports of doctors if you make enquiries, enquire of your friends, enquire about a doctor at a shop, or shops, and if you find you cannot get on with the first doctor, well, good gracious me, there are plenty of them. Try another!

You should be warned, though, that when you have found a good general practitioner—hang on to him, he's worth his weight in gold and platters of diamonds. When you have your good general practitioner let him tell you if you need the services of a specialist. He knows the human body, its functions, and its malfunctions better than you do. So get to know a good general practitioner, get to know him and trust him, tell him all your symptoms.

Never use your druggist as a prescribing agency. A druggist may be exceptionally good as a druggist, but he is not necessarily qualified to be a general practitioner. So your doctor should be the one to diagnose and the one to prescribe, and the druggist is the one who fills the prescription.

I am going to make myself frightfully unpopular here. I am going to advise you that if you are ill, definitely your best choice is an orthodox, common or garden general practitioner. Avoid spiritualistic healers and others who do not have scientific training because, just for a simple example, it is utterly easy to hypnotise a person into believing that he does not have such-and-such an illness or such-and-such a symptom. You can 'cure' that illness, but unless you know enough about bodies and medicine to get down to basics you can easily start up a far worse illness. By meddling with spiritualistic stuff, or hypnotic healers who do not have medical training, you can turn an ordinary harmless lump into cancerous tissue. So be very sure that if you are ill you go to an orthodox general practitioner who has the necessary medical training.

Many people are bemused by the different medical

specialities, so for your reference let us mention just a few of the more common ones in alphabetical order.

ALLERGY is the study of altered reactions of the body to certain substances.
ANESTHESIOLOGY is the medical specialty of administering anaesthetics, in other words, killing the pain.
DERMATOLOGY deals with skin diseases.
ENDOCRINOLOGY relates to the study of the glands and their internal secretions.
GASTROENTEROLOGY relates to stomach and intestines.
HEMATOLOGY is the science of the blood.
NEUROLOGY deals with the nervous system.

It's hardly worth mentioning Obstetrics and Gynaecology or Ophthalmology, because everyone knows that the first is to deal with babies, etc., or rather their production, the second with female diseases in general, and Ophthalmology deals with eye troubles.

The nurse in the hospital says 'E.N.T.' meaning Ear, Nose, and Throat. If she was correct or highbrow, she would say, 'Otology, Laryngology, and Rhinology.'

PEDIATRICS is the medical science of dealing with children's diseases.

Again, anyone knows what Physiatry is, which is not to be confused with Psychiatry. Physiatry is the science of physical reconditioning and rehabilitation.

The Proctologist could almost get an advanced Naval rank, because unkind people refer to the Proctologist as the 'Rear Admiral' because he inspects the rear. That is diseases of the anus and rectum.

PSYCHIATRY is the science of mental diseases.
RADIOLOGY is X-ray work.
THORACIC surgery is surgery within the chest cavity.
UROLOGY—for our last one—which deals with anything to do with the urogenital tract, that is the kidneys, the bladder, and the sex organs.

So, now you have some nice big words, and you know what your general practitioner means if he should tell you or one of your friends that you should see a 'So-and-So'.

CHAPTER FOUR

THE night was cold, bitterly cold. On the shrubs across the road a thin layer of snow glistened and sparkled, giving a Christmas cake effect to little plants and small apple trees. Further across a small garden patch, a heavy diesel locomotive chugged and roared away as it waited for a distant signal to give the 'All Clear' so that it could drag its long, long line of freight cars on to New York carrying thousands of new automobiles from Detroit, across Canada, and again into the U.S.A.

Further up the hill a horrendous clamour erupted upon the shuddering air as a recorded carillon of bells blasted from a modern church steeple with such volume that everything seemed to tremble and crouch in fright. From the nearby hotel came the sounds of late-night revelry as tipplers celebrated or bemoaned their luck that day at the local race-track. Well-known bookies were smiling with joy, for that day there had been a 'killing'. The talk came clearly, the clatter of bottles and glasses was sharp upon the night air, and the rattle and tinkle of the cash registers were a continual reminder that someone, at least, was enjoying prosperity.

Across the long bridge spanning the railroad tracks people returning from late duty in shops and factories sped homeward in gay abandon, oblivious of the risk of police speed traps. Further to the left a neon sign blinked on and off, with mindless robotic regularity, tinging the snow, now blood red then green then red again.

In the frosty air the stars shone hard and clear, not a wisp of cloud obscured the sky, not a strand of smoke impeded the light from the now rising moon. The air was crisp, crisp, and almost tinkling with a layer of frost.

The old man, sitting motionless in the cheap and shaky wheelchair, suddenly moved and pushed the window wide open. The chilly air was like a tonic, like a breath of new life after the heat of the day, and the old man was immune to the cold but could not stand the heat. Sitting in the wheelchair in his pyjamas, for the night was advanced, he wheeled his chair to a covered object beside the window. Taking off the cloth covering, revealed a powerful telescope. Quickly pushing it in position, he prepared to focus on the little points of light such illimitable distance away.

'Do you want to freeze us all to death?' mildly enquired a voice from another room.

'This is not cold,' said the old man. 'Tonight I think we shall be able to see the Rings of Saturn very clearly. Do you want to come and look?'

For a moment there was a rustling and a bustling, and then, first a chink, and then a growing amount of light as a door was opened in back of the old man's room. Mrs. Old Man came through and shut the door behind her. She, poor soul, was well wrapped up, and even had a blanket over an overcoat around her shoulders. The old man bent over his telescope, staring to focus in the general direction of the planet Saturn.

Suddenly his attention was distracted by something. Quickly moving the telescope he re-focused on something, and tensed with rigid concentration.

'What is it, what is it?' asked Mrs. Old Man. 'Is it an aeroplane?'

The old man sat silent, his fingers moving over the focusing of the telescope. 'Quick, quick,' he said, 'be ready to put your eye here as soon as I move. This is something you've wanted to see. Ready?!'

'Yes!' said Mrs. Old Man, and got ready to look as soon as the old man himself had got his head out of the way. She peered through the telescope, up into the night sky, following the path of a long bar like a dumb-bell, sliding across the sky, a dumb-bell lit at both ends, and between the two lights a whole series of flickering, blinking, twinkling, ever-changing colours. She breathed hard, 'I've never seen anything like this!' she exclaimed. But then, as she looked, the object came close overhead, and with the telescope she was looking right up underneath. A thing like a door opened in the object, and from the door came a number of bright vehicles, glistening globes. They shot out of what was obviously a mother-ship, and then extinguished their lights and disappeared in all directions. The mother-ship then extinguished her lights, hovered for a moment or two, and then shot heavenwards and was seen in dark silhouette diminishing in size against the bright night sky.

The noise continued from the hotel. No one had been disturbed. Cars continued to speed across the railroad bridge. The returning travellers were too intent upon their driving. In the cab of the great diesel locomotive the engineer smoked his cigar and read his newspaper by the cab light, oblivious of the great ship which was there for him, and for anyone else, to see. To the left the mindless, robotic neon sign changed from green to red, to green and red again. The world went about its business, looking down at the works of Man, ignoring the strange things that flew in the night skies as they had flown for centuries past, and would fly for years to come until, in the end, the people from space decide to land on this Earth once again.

They have been here before, you know. Earth is like a colony, Earth is a testing ground, a seeding place where different types are put together so that the Gardeners of Space can see how they get on together. Don't believe all the rot about God being dead. God is very much alive, and God is using this Earth as a testing ground, and letting little humans learn upon Earth for the much greater things that will happen in the life to come.

The little town, perched sleepily on the side of the placid river, basked in the late afternoon sun. Shoppers slowly meandered along the street, window-gazing first, and then having a not too strenuous mental fight that they should decide what could be afforded and what could not.

The stores and the supermarkets were not at all crowded for this was a slack day in the shopping week, but people wandered about more as an excuse to be out in the sunshine.

Down by the coal wharf men were unenthusiastically dealing with the self-unloader of a coal ship moored alongside. There came the desultory and staccato noise of a bulldozer shovelling mounds of coal, ready to be loaded into an endless stream of trucks and taken to great factories nearby.

Just off the parking lot a mongrel dog of indefinable ancestry pawed lethargically among the refuse. A well-aimed potato caught him on the flank and he rushed off howling, showing the only turn of speed seen in the little town that day.

Down by the river's edge some boys were paddling —without taking their shoes and socks off! They had an old wrecked boat, with the timbers rotten and worm-eaten, and they were lazily engaged in play having to do with Morgan the Pirate. On the other side of the street the man in the radio shop was just changing a record, giving a welcome relief from the blasting volume of sound which normally poured from that area.

Someone, possibly a housewife, possibly a farmer from further inland, gazed without curiosity up into the sky wondering, no doubt, if the weather would keep up so that the crops could be harvested. Gazed up—and froze into shocked immobility. Passers-by looked at him for a moment, and smiled to themselves, then turned and looked up into the sky. They too became shocked. More and more people gazed up into the hot sky, gazing, gesticulating, pointing, a babble of sound arose. Cars screeched to a halt, and drivers and passengers poured out to look upwards.

From the river's bank the boys stopped their play and looked up. One tripped and fell backwards into the water filling the old wrecked boat. Yelling with alarm, he leaped to his feet and he and his companions raced for the market square with water squelching from their shoes, and with the one boy dripping water from the seat of his pants.

A man dashed into a house, and was gone but a moment before returning with a pair of binoculars. Feverishly he put them to his eyes and with trembling fingers focused. The babble of talk increased. Quickly the glasses were snatched from him and passed from one person to another as they all gazed up.

High in the sky, beyond the height at which aircraft would fly, there hovered a large silver pear-shaped object, with the larger part pointing down and the smaller part pointing up. It hovered there, huge and in some alien way, menacing. 'That's not a balloon!' said one man who had recently returned from the Air Force. 'If it was a balloon the larger part would be at the top instead of at the bottom.'

'Yes!' exclaimed another, 'And it would be drifting with the wind. Look at those high alto-stratus clouds passing by it, and yet IT is stationary.'

The little town buzzed with consternation and speculation. High above, unmoving, inscrutable, hovered the enigmatic object. Never varying in position, making no motion, no movement of any kind. Slowly the day came to a close with the object there as though glued to a picture of the heavens itself, there, unmoving, unchanging. The moon came up and shone across the countryside, and above in the moonlight the object loitered. With the first early dawn it was still there. People who were preparing to go to work looked out of their windows. The object was still there as if a fixture, and then, suddenly, it moved. Faster and faster it went, straight up, straight up into space, and disappeared.

Yes, you know, there are people in space ships who are watching this world. Watching to see what happens. 'Well, why do they not come and talk to us like sensible people would?' you may ask, but the only reply is that they are being sensible. Humans try to shoot them, and try in any way to harm these U.F.O.s, and if the U.F.O.s, or rather the people within them, have the intelligence to cross space, then they have the intelligence to make apparatus which can listen to Earth radio and Earth television, and if they watch Earth television—well, then they will think they have come to some vast mental home, because what could be more insane than the television programmes which are foisted on a suffering public? Television programmes which glorify the unclean, which glorify the criminal, which teach sex in the wrong way, in the worst possible way, which teach people that only self-gain and sex matters.

Would you dive into a fish tank that you could discuss things with some worms at the bottom of the tank? Or would you go to a colony of ants labouring in one of these glass tanks designed to show the work of the ants? Would you go in there and talk with ants, or with any of these lesser creatures? Would you go into some glass hothouse and talk to some experimental plants, ask them how they are doing, saying, 'Take me to your leader?' No! You would watch, and if an ant bit you you'd say, 'Spiteful little things, aren't they?' And be careful that you didn't get bitten in the future.

So the people of space, whose one-year-old children would know more than the wisest man on this Earth, just watch over this colony.

A very few years ago I lived in Montevideo, the capital of Uruguay, a country which in South America lies between Argentina and Brazil. Montevideo is upon the River Plate and ships of the world pass by going to Rio de Janeiro or to Buenos Aires, or come into the Port of Montevideo. From my ninth floor apartment I could look out across the River, right out to the South Atlantic beyond the confines of the River. There were no obstacles, no obstructions, to the view.

Night after night my family and I used to watch U.F.O.s coming from the direction of the South Pole straight over our apartment building, and coming lower so that they could alight in the Matto Grosso of Brazil. Night after night, with unvarying regularity, these U.F.O.s came. They were seen not just by us, but by a multitude of people, and in Argentina they are officially recognised as Unknown Flying Objects. The Argentine Government are well aware that these things are not the product of hysteria or a fevered imagination, they are aware that U.F.O.s are of surpassing reality.

The day we landed in Buenos Aires a U.F.O. came in and actually alighted at the main airport. It stayed for several minutes at the end of a runway, and then took off at fantastic speed. I was about to say that all this can be read in the press reports, but that is no proof of the truth of it because too often the press alter things to suit themselves or to get more readers, and I have no faith whatever in anything which is printed in the daily press. So, instead, I will say that this U.F.O. landing is the subject of an Argentinian Government Report.

Having seen these U.F.O.s night after night, and seen how they can change course and manoeuvre, I state emphatically that these were not satellites flashing across the sky. The times that satellites can be seen varies, and is known to the minute; the times that we saw these other things were different, and in addition we have also seen the satellites. The night sky of Montevideo is remarkably clear, and I had a very high-power telescope of the type used by the Swiss Customs Officials which ranged from forty magnification up to three hundred and fifty.

This world is under observation, but we need not be upset by that. It is sad indeed that so many people always fear that those who observe wish to do harm. They do not, they wish to do good. Remember that there are ages and ages going back into history, and various civilisations and cultures have appeared and disappeared almost without trace. Remember the civilisation of Sumeria, and the great civilisation of Minoa. Who has been able to explain the enigmatic statues of Easter Island? Yes, someone once tried to and wrote a sort of a book about it, but it's not necessarily accurate, you know. Or, if you want to go to another stage, how about the Maya people? Can anyone say what happened to the Mayan civilisation?

Each of these civilisations was a fresh culture placed upon the Earth to liven up stock which had become dull and, what I can only term, 'denatured'.

There is also a very, very ancient theory, or legend, that countless years ago a space ship came to this Earth and something went wrong with the ship, it could not take off. So the people aboard, men, women, and children, were marooned here, and they started another form of civilisation.

It is extremely fortunate that the Hebrew Books of the Old Testament had been translated into Greek long before Christians came upon the scene, because the early Christians, just like the present-day ones, tried to alter things to their own gain. We can, then, find out a lot about ancient history from the Hebrew Books which have not been tampered with by Christianity, but even they leave us uninformed about the Mayas, the Easter Islands, and the Etruscans. These were civilisations which flourished more than 3000 years B.C. We can know that because Egyptian hieroglyphs can be traced back to the year 3000 B.C., and some of these, traced upon temple walls and in tombs, give information about earlier and very great civilisations. Unfortunately around about two hundred years after the start of Christianity knowledge of much of this had been lost because of the manner in which Christians altered history to suit themselves, and because, with the rise in power of Christianity, Egyptian temples were closed down and no longer were there educated priests who could understand the hieroglyphs. And so for several hundred years history remained in darkness.

Later research indicates that many thousands of years ago a great Race suddenly appeared 'in the Land of the Two Rivers'. These people, now known to us as the Sumerians, have left little of their recorded history. Actually, according to the Akashic Record, the Gardeners of the Earth decided that the 'stock' on Earth was becoming weakened by inbreeding, and so they placed upon the Earth others who also had to learn. These others are known to us as the Sumerians, and a particular branch of the Sumerians —almost like a family—became the Semites, and they in their turn became the earliest form of Hebrews. But that was about 2000 B.C.

The Kingdom of Sumeria was a truly mighty kingdom, and brought to this Earth many advancements in culture and science, and many different plants. Certain branches of the Sumerian culture left the founding city and moved to Mesopotamia in round about the year 4000 B.C. In addition they bred and gradually populated areas of high culture. It is interesting to know that when Abraham moved with his herds from the City of Ur in Mesopotamia and went to Palestine, he and those with him brought legends which had been family history for thousands of years. They brought with them stories of the Garden of Eden, a land which lay between the Tigris and the Euphrates. This had been the common ground of many, many tribes and people who had been expanding—as their populations increased—over what is known as the Middle East. 'Eden', by the way, actually means 'a plain'. The Book of Genesis was merely a digest of stories which had been told by the people of Mesopotamia for several thousand years.

Eventually civilisations became absorbed. So it was that the Sumerian civilisation, having leavened the stock of Earth, became absorbed and lost within the great mass of Earth people. And so, in different parts of the world and in different times, other 'leavening cultures' had to be set down, such as the Etruscans, the Minoans, the Mayas, and the Easter Island people.

According to the old legends the Twelve Tribes of Israel do not altogether refer to the people of Earth, but instead mean one tribe which was the original people of the Earth, and the eleven 'tribes', or cultures, which were put down here to leaven the original which was becoming weakened by inbreeding.

Consider, for your own amusement, various tribes; the black people, the yellow people, the white people, and so on. Now which do you think is the original

Earth inhabitant and which are descended from the Mayas, the Sumerians, the Etruscans, and others? It makes interesting speculation. But there is no need to speculate because, I tell you very seriously, that if you will practise what I have tried to show you in all my books, you can do astral travel. And if you can do astral travel you can know what is happening, and what has happened, through the Akashic Record. The Akashic Record is no television show where we are interrupted by 'a few words from our sponsor'; here we have the utter truth, here we have absolute exactitude. History as it was, not as it was re-written to suit some dictator who did not like the truth of his early life, for example.

By visiting the Hall of the Akashic Record you can find the truth about the Dead Sea Scrolls, those Scrolls which were found in 1947 in certain caves by the Dead Sea in a district called Qumran. This collection of Scrolls belonged to a certain Order of Jews who, in many ways, resembled Christians. They had a Man at the head who was known as the Teacher of the Rightful Way. He was known as the Suffering Son of God, who was born to suffer and die for humanity. According to the Scrolls He had been tortured and crucified, but would rise again.

Now, you might think that this refers to the Leader of Christianity, Jesus. But this Teacher of the Rightful Way lived at least a hundred and fifty years before Jesus came to the Earth. The evidence is definite, the evidence is absolutely precise. The Scrolls themselves were part of a Library of this particular Jewish sect, and the Library had been endangered by the Romans, and some of the Jewish monks had hidden certain Scrolls, probably the only ones that they had time to save.

There are various ways in which science can determine the age of any reputably antique object, and these Scrolls have been subjected to those tests, and the tests indicate that they are about five hundred years older than Christianity. There is no possibility that they were written after the advent of Christianity. It follows from this that it would pay to have a really sound investigation into the Bible and all religious papers, because the Bible has been translated and re-translated many, many times, and even to the experts many of the things in the Bible cannot be explained. If only one could overcome religious bias, religious prejudice, and discuss things openly, one could get down to basic facts and the history of the world could be set right. There is, I repeat, a good way, and that is to consult the Akashic Record. Now, it is possible for you to do this if you first become proficient in astral travel, but if anyone tells you that he or she will go into the astral for you and look at the Akashic Record provided you pay him or her a certain sum of money, consider him to be a fake, because these things are not done for money.

I hope I have said enough in this chapter to indicate that the U.F.O.s are real, and they are not a menace to anyone on this Earth. The U.F.O.s are merely the Gardeners of the Earth who come here from time to time to see what is happening to their stock, and they have been here so much more frequently, and in much greater numbers recently because mankind has been playing around with atomic bombs, and risking blowing up the whole dump.

What a terrible commotion there has been about U.F.O.s, hasn't there? Yet, U.F.O.s are mentioned very extensively in the Greek Legends and in the Religious Books of many different forms of religious belief. In the Bible U.F.O.s are mentioned, and there are many reports in ancient monasteries, such as, 'When the monks were sat down to lunch at midday, having their first meal of meat for many weeks, a strange aerial object came over and panicked the good Brothers.'

U.F.O.s have been showing increasing activity during the past fifty or sixty years because the people of Earth have been showing increased hostility towards each other; think of the first Great War, think of the second Great War in which pilots of all nations saw what they called 'Foo Fighters', which were indisputably U.F.O.s watching the progress of battles. Then take the matter of airline pilots. It doesn't matter which airline, it doesn't matter which country, because airline pilots all over the world have seen many strange and even possibly frightening U.F.O.s. They have talked about it extensively, too, but in many Western countries there is a heavy censorship about such things. Fortunate it is, too, or the press, with their usual distortion, would twist everything up and make the harmless into something horrendous.

It has usually been said, 'Oh, well, if there are U.F.O.s why have not astronomers seen them?' The answer is that astronomers have seen them, and have photographed them, but again there is such a censorship that people in prominent positions are afraid to talk about things they have seen. They are afraid to talk for fear of getting into trouble with the authorities who do not want the truth known. They are afraid to talk because they fear that their professional integrity will seem to be in doubt, for people who have not seen U.F.O.s are extremely virulent in their hatred for those who have.

So the pilots who fly the airlines, whether in a commercial capacity or in connection with the armed forces, have seen and will continue to see U.F.O.s but until the moronic governments of the world change their attitudes, not much will be heard of those sightings. The Argentine Government is surely one of the most enlightened in that they officially recognise the existence of U.F.O.s. They were, in fact, the first country in the world to recognise U.F.O.s as actualities. Other countries are afraid to permit any accurate information for various reasons. In the first case, the Christian belief seems to be that Man is made in the image of God, and, as nothing is greater than God nothing can be greater than Man who is made in the image of God. And so if there is some sort of creature who can make a space ship which can go through space, visiting different worlds, then that must be hushed up because the creature may not be in the shape of Man. It's all distorted reasoning, but things will change in the not too distant future.

Then the military clique cannot acknowledge the existence of U.F.O.s because to do so would be to admit that there is something more powerful than the military clique. The Russian dictators, for example, could not admit the existence of these U.F.O.s because to do so would lessen their own stature in the eyes of their people. Now all the good little Commies —if there are any good Commies—think that the leaders in Moscow are omnipotent, infallible, and the most wondrous things that ever appeared on Earth. So if a little green man, three or four feet high, should be able to travel from world to world, and not all the resources of the great Moscow leaders could shoot down the little green man, then it would show that the little green man is more important than the Communist powers, and that would never do for the Communists. So, everything about U.F.O.s is banned.

People also say that if there were U.F.O.s, the astronauts or cosmonauts or whatever they call themselves would have seen them. But that's not at all accurate, you know; consider this—these fellows who have been in space have just been up a bit higher than any other humans on Earth. They have not really been in space, they have just been in a rarefied atmosphere. They are not in space until they go behind the Van Allen belts of radiation, and they are not truly in space until they have gone to the Moon and come back. Further, saying that there are no

U.F.O.s because if there had been the space men would have seen them, is much the same as saying, as you gaze out on the ocean, that there are no fish in the ocean, if there were you could see them! You get chilly looking fellows who sit by the side of the sea for hours trying to catch a fish. It's a full-time job with them—trying to catch a fish. And yet there are millions of fish in the sea. They are hard to see, though, aren't they, if you just take a glimpse at the ocean? In the same way, if you are shot up into the rarefied atmosphere a hundred or so miles above the surface of the Earth, and you look out of a little hole in your tin can—well, you don't see a whole procession of U.F.O.s. For one thing you are too uncomfortable, and secondly you don't have much of a view there.

But wait a minute, though. If you have listened-in to the astronauts radioing back to Earth you will have heard, or remembered that there have been references to these U.F.O.s seen by astronauts, but in all future re-plays that reference has been carefully censored and deleted. The astronaut in the enthusiasm of the moment has mentioned U.F.O.s. And also mentioned photographing U.F.O.s, and yet in all later reports such references have been denied.

It seems, then, that we are up against quite a bad plot, a plot to conceal a knowledge of what circles the Earth. A plot to conceal the very real existence of U.F.O.s. In the press and in various pseudo-scientific journals there have been references to U.F.O.s in the most scarey terms, how wicked these things are, how dangerous, and how they do this or that. And how they have got a tremendous plot to take over the Earth. Don't believe a word of it! If the U.F.O. people had wanted to take over the Earth they could have done it centuries ago. The whole point is, they are AFRAID that they will have to take over the Earth (and they do not want to) if the Earth goes on releasing too much hard atomic radiation.

These spacemen are the Gardeners of the Earth. They are trying to save the Earth from the Earth people—and what a time they are having! There are reports of many different types of U.F.O.s. Well, of course there are! There are many different types of aircraft upon the Earth. You can, for example, have a glider without any engine. You can have a monoplane or a biplane. You can have a one-seater aircraft or a two-hundred-plus-seater aircraft, and if you don't want noisy aircraft then presumably you could get a spherical gas balloon or one of those very interesting things made by Goodyear. So, if you had a procession of these contraptions flying over darkest Africa, the people there would be most amazed at the variety, and would no doubt think that they came from different cultures. In the same way, because some space craft are round, or ellipse shaped, or cigar shaped, or dumb-bell shaped, the uninformed person thinks they must come from different planets. Possibly some of them do, but it doesn't matter in the slightest because they are not belligerent, they are not hostile. They are manned by quite benevolent people.

Most of these U.F.O.s are of the same 'polarity' as the people of the Earth, and so they can, if they wish, alight on the surface of the Earth or dive beneath the surface of the sea. But another type of U.F.O. comes from the 'negative' side and cannot come close to the Earth—perhaps I should say cannot come close to the Earth's surface—without disintegrating in a violent explosion with a tremendous clap of thunder, because these particular U.F.O.s come from the world of anti-matter. That is, the opposite type of world from this. Everything, you know, has its equal and opposite. You can say that there is a sex thing in planets, one is male and the other is female, one is positive and the other is negative, one is matter and the other is anti-matter. So when you get reports of a tremendous explosion or see a vast fireball plunging to Earth and excavating a huge crater, you may guess that a U.F.O. from an anti-matter world has come here and crashed.

There have been reports of so-called 'hostile' acts by U.F.O.s. People, we are told, have been kidnapped. But do we have any proof whatever that anyone has really been harmed? After all, if you have a Zoo and you want to examine a specimen, you pick up a specimen and bear it away. You examine it. You might test its blood, you may test its breath content, you could X-ray it and weigh it and measure it. No doubt all those things would appear to be very frightening and very tormenting to the ignorant animal involved. But the animal, when carefully replaced, is none the worse for this weighing and measuring, none the worse at all. In the same way, a gardener can examine a plant. He doesn't hurt the plant, he is not there to hurt plants, he is there to make them grow, make them better. So he examines the plant to see what can be done to improve it. In the same way the Gardeners of the Earth occasionally pick up a specimen, a man or a woman. Well, all right, so they measure a human, examine him or her, do a few tests, and then put the human back into the human surroundings. And he or she is none the worse off for it, it's only because they are scared silly that they think they are any the worse off. Usually they are so frightened that they concoct the most horrible tales about what happened to them, when, actually, nothing unusual whatever happened.

This world is being watched, and it has been watched since long, long before the dinosaurs thundered across the face of this Earth. The world is being watched, and it will be watched for quite a time, and eventually the people of space will come down here. Not as tormentors, not as slave-owners, but as benevolent teachers or guides. Various countries now send what they call a Peace Corps to what are alleged to be under-developed countries. These Peace Corps people —who usually are in need of some form of excitement, or they can't get some other type of job—go out into jungles and teach 'backward' people the things which they really do not need to know. Things which give them false ideas and false values. They get shown a film of perhaps some film star's marvellous palace in Hollywood and then they all get the idea that if they become Christians, or Peace Corps Patrons, they also will have such a marvellous edifice in which to live, complete with swimming pool and naked dancing girls.

When the people from space come here they will not behave like that. They will show people by example how they should go on, show them that wars are not necessary, show them a true religion which can be expressed in the words, 'Do as you would be done by.'

Before much longer governments of the world will have to tell the truth about U.F.O.s, will have to tell about peoples from outer space. They know already, but they really are scared to let the public know. But the sooner they do let the public know, the sooner it will be possible to adjust, to prepare, and to avoid any untoward incidents when our Gardeners return to this world. People write to me about the so-called 'Men in Black'. Well, that is newspaper, or journalistic license. It just means that there are outer space people here upon the Earth observing, recording, and planning. They are not here to cause trouble for anyone. They are here so that they may gain information with which they can best plan how to help the people of the Earth. Unfortunately too many Earth people react like mad animals, and if they think they are being attacked they go berserk. If one of these 'Men in Black' (who may be dressed in any colour!) is attacked, then obviously he has to defend himself. But unfortunately his defence is often distorted to appear to be an original attack when it's nothing of the sort.

There are many types of U.F.O.s. There are many shapes and sizes of people within those U.F.O.s, but these people share one thing in common; they have lived a long time, longer than the people of Earth, and they have learned much. They have learned that warfare is childishness. They have learned that it is far better for people to get on together without all the quarrelling. They have learned that Earth has apparently gone mad, and they want to do something to bring the people of Earth back to sanity, and to stop excessive atomic radiation. And if they cannot stop that peacefully, then Earth will have to be in quarantine for centuries to come, and that would hold up the spiritual development of great masses of people here.

So, in conclusion, do not fear U.F.O.s, for there is nothing to fear. Instead, open your mind to the knowledge that before too long the people of this Earth will have visitors from space who will not be belligerent but who will try to help us as we should help others.

CHAPTER FIVE

IF you could see the letters I receive, and keep on seeing them over more than a decade, you would come to one inescapable conclusion; readers are queer people! Not YOU, of course, but all the other readers, or rather some of them, because some are very, very nice indeed.

One constant type of comment I get is that I should send more copies of my books free to Public Libraries. People write in and tell me they cannot afford the price for my paperback books, and they can only read, they tell me, if I supply them free to Libraries.

Well, I am not much in favour of that idea. An Author makes his only living from royalties on books. If I write a book I get ten per cent of the profit, ten per cent in some countries, seven per cent in others, and always on the lowest selling price. If a book is sent from England—where it is very low priced—to America, where it has to bear the cost of carriage, etc., I do not get the royalties on the higher American price. I get the royalties on the lower English price—royalties on the profit, mind you, after all expenses have been taken off by the Publisher. I also have to pay an Agent, or two Agents, and sometimes from my ten per cent I have to pay twenty per cent in Agent's fees. Then there are taxes, and an Author, all too frequently, encounters double taxation. That is, he pays full tax in one country, and then has to pay tax on the same sum in another country. And, believe me, that knocks all the gilt off the gingerbread, and you end up with hardly any 'bread' at all.

In addition I have to pay quite a lot of other things—stationery, envelopes, stamps. And let me remind you, also, that an Author who answers letters is the worst paid man in the world. A buck navvy who leisurely digs a hole in a road is paid for his work, he is paid for his time. A lawyer is paid for his time and his skill, so is a doctor. But people write to an Author, actually demanding this or that service, or this or that gift, and nine times out of ten they do not even enclose return postage. If they do it is all too frequently postage from another country. For example, people in America who send stamped addressed envelopes, put American stamps on which, of course, cannot be used in a Sovereign State such as Canada. So what is one to do then? Pay the cost of the stationery, the printing of the letter heading? Some letters have to be typed; that again costs money. And the postage has to be met. So, as you will agree, people write to an Author and expect all for nothing. I actually had a person write to me and tell me that he had bought one of my books; as such he was entitled to my whole services, he told me. He said that he had read in the back of the book that I was asking people to write to me. It never entered his head that I was asking people NOT to write to me!

As an Author I depend upon royalties, and if people borrow books from the Public Library I do not get any payment. And yet the ones who borrow from a Public Library are the ones who are most demanding in their questions and requirements. I have had a person write to me and tell me that she had read one of my books, and 'you may now send me complimentary autographed copies of all your books, and I want an autographed photograph of you'. What would you reply to that, dear Reader?

One gets various amusing incidents also. I am

highly amused at the behaviour of a little group of people in Adelaide, Australia. I call them the 'Apes of Adelaide'. These are a little gang who have been in trouble, it seems, with the police. Now I had someone write to me, telling me various things in confidence, and asking did I recommend these people. I wrote back and said, No, I did not. Since then I have had dozens of obscene letters from these people, and every so often I get, perhaps, nine or ten which say, 'I hereby disconnect from you.' It strikes me as rather amusing because we have never been connected, so how can one disconnect that which has never been connected? I am informed that this gang have a requirement now that anyone who joins them (poor unfortunate soul!) has to put a name, any name, to one of these pre-typed slips and mail it off to me. Well, it's good for the postal authorities. It's also very good for the police, because I mail the whole lot back to the police at Adelaide, complete with the envelopes, so they can keep a file of these names and the handwriting, as those police have informed me they are investigating this little gang. I await developments with the greatest of interest. So—Apes of Adelaide—I send you my greetings, and I am still puzzled how we can be disconnected when we have never been connected.

Another person in Vancouver wrote to a friend of his (who promptly informed me!) saying that 'Lobsang Rampa could not be genuine because in one of his books he says he does not like the Irish tax collector'!

Yet another from Vancouver heard that I was poor, very poor, and this good lady promptly said that I was obviously a fake if I was poor, because if I was genuine money would come to me and I would be a millionaire. It did not occur to her, apparently, that there are some things more valuable than gold or diamonds. Actually, she is barking up the wrong tree, because a person who really can help others in the occult does not make a charge, he does not put things on a commercial basis. If people want to make a gift of money to help out—well, that is acceptable, but such people are rarer than hen's teeth.

There are compensations, though. There are very many nice people who write. I have had a letter telling me that a noted 'Seer' is of the opinion, and has so stated publicly, that 'Lobsang Rampa has done more for the Occult world than any other person on or off the Earth'. Quite a nice compliment, eh? Certainly it is one which I very greatly appreciate because, whatever some people think, I am trying to do a job in helping others know what all this is about, in this life and after this life.

Yes, there are compensations, there are good people. More than a decade ago, when I first came to Canada, I had a letter from a woman and by psychometry I judged that this was a nice person and genuine. She asked if she could come and see me. Well, at that time I had a car—now I have a wheelchair, and I can't afford a car—so I decided that I would drive to her house and just give her a surprise. I did so, and I found a very nice woman indeed. Mrs. Valeria Sorock. During the past ten years the friendship and personal liking between her and my family and I has grown to its present stage that she is accepted, not just as a friend, not just as someone who writes, but as one of the family. She writes, but we have met her on very many occasions, and wherever we have lived in Canada she has visited us. She even visited us when we were in Montevideo, in the country of Uruguay.

Last night I had a really long-distance call from Mrs. Valeria Sorock, a telephone call because those unmentionable mail men are on strike here in Canada. So Mrs. Sorock made this telephone call, and she said that as I was writing another book she would like to have a few questions answered. So I wrote down her questions and I told her that I would answer her in this book if she agreed to have her name as the one asking the questions. By the way, Mrs. Sorock is the perfectionist in English who shudders so violently when she reads my distorted form of prose, and sometimes when she peruses proofs and sees grammatical errors—well, she turns positively pale! But now, let us send a greeting to Mrs. Valeria Sorock and deal with her questions.

The first question is: 'How can one overcome fear?'

Fear? You must know what you fear. What DO you fear? Do you fear the Unknown? Until you know what it is that you fear you cannot do anything about it. Fear is a harmful thing, it is a shameful thing, it is a thing which stultifies progress. How to overcome fear; the best way is to think of that thing which you fear. Think about it from all angles. What is it? Why should it affect you? What do you think it can do to you? Is it going to injure you physically? Is it going to injure you financially? Will it matter in fifty year's time?

If you carefully analyse your feelings, if you carefully go into the subject of this 'Why-do-I-fear?' you will surely come to realise that there is nothing to fear. I have yet to find anything which can make one fear if one really goes into the matter.

Do you fear the police, or our old enemy the Tax Collector? Do you fear things in the astral world? Well, there's no need to because I state most definitely that if you analyse this object, or this condition, or this circumstance which causes you to experience fear, you will see that it is a harmless thing after all.

Do you fear poverty? Then what DO you fear? Take it out of its dark closet. Is it your 'skeleton in the closet'? Take it out, dust off the cobwebs, and look at the problem from all angles. You will find that fear vanishes, and always remember that if you do not fear, then nothing in this world or off this world can harm you. And believe me when I say that people off this world are a lot kinder than the people on this world.

Now, we come to the second question, which is: 'How does one know when one is doing right?'

Every person, every entity on this world or off this world has a built-in 'censor', a part of the mind which enables a person to know if he or she is doing right. If a person gets drunk or under the influence of drugs, the censor is temporarily stunned, and the behaviour of a person who is drunk or is under the influence of drugs can be very bad, and can be far worse than would be the case if the person's personal censor was in working order.

You can always tell when you are doing right. You feel right. If you are doing wrong, then you have an uneasy feeling that something is not as it should be. The best way to be sure of knowing if you are doing right or doing wrong is to practise meditation. If you wrap yourself in your meditation robe you insulate yourself from the rest of the world, and your astral form can become disengaged from outside influence and can give you enlightenment direct from the Overself. If you meditate, you see, it's not just a lump of protoplasm giving you ideas; when you meditate you actually receive confirmation of your good or bad from your Overself. And so I say to you—if you are in doubt, meditate, and then you will know the truth.

Mrs. Sorock, now you have asked me something! You ask, 'How can one develop Extra Sensory Powers?'

Well, sad to say some people never do. Just the same as some people can never paint a picture, some people cannot sing a song—or if they do they are soon told to shut up! Some people cannot do E.S.P. because they are so sure that they cannot do E.S.P. But if one is willing to try, E.S.P. is easy. You cannot normally do the whole bunch, you know; telekinesis, telepathy, clairvoyance, clairaudience, psychometry, and the whole lot. If you've been trained in E.S.P. from your seventh year up, then you can do it.

But, assume now that you want to learn to do some form of E.S.P. We have to specify something, so let us say psychometry is your choice. You are anxious to practise psychometry. Well, you have to have exercises just as if you are learning to play the piano, you practise the scales, and you go on practising those silly scales day after day, week after week. And even when you are an accomplished musician, you still have to practise scales.

Let us get back, though, to this psychometry. You want to learn psychometry so the best thing to do is to have a week or two just saying to yourself in a positive manner that you ARE going to be proficient at psychometry (or clairvoyance or clairaudience, or whatever it is you wish). You visualise yourself putting your hand, usually the left hand, on an object, and you visualise yourself getting a clear picture, or a clear impression about that object.

For one or two weeks, then, you fill your waking hours with thoughts that you are definitely going to do this. Then, after perhaps fourteen days, you wait until the mailman has been, and you take a letter which he has delivered, and you just gently rest your left hand upon it—before you open it, of course. Rest your left hand upon it. Close your eyes, and sit in any relaxed position. Let yourself imagine (later it will really be so) that you can feel some strange influence coming out from the envelope and tickling the palm of your hand and your fingers.

By this time you should be getting some sort of sensation in your left hand. Well, just try to let your mind go blank, and see what sort of impression you get. First it will be crude, it will be utterly rudimentary. You can classify the letter as 'good' or 'bad'. You can classify it as 'friendly' or 'unfriendly'. Then open your letter and read it, and see if your impression was correct. If you were correct then you will succeed rapidly, because nothing succeeds like success.

First of all try with just this one letter, that is on one day. Next day try two or three letters, or, if you wish, stick to one only, but this time try to 'feel' what the letter is about. Persevere with it, and as you succeed you will go on to much better things.

When you are proficient in psychometry—and it only takes practice—you will be able to actually visualise, or even actually see the person who wrote the letter, and you will know the gist of it without opening the envelope. It is a simple matter, and it merely needs practice. If you are learning to touch-type and you peek at the keys, you are putting yourself back. You have to learn to type without looking at the keys, and as you make progress and hit the right keys in the right sequence, you get confidence and you can go faster. It's the same with psychometry; as you make correct 'guesses', which are really correct impressions, it strengthens your confidence, and with strengthened confidence you find that you are progressing faster and faster and becoming more and more accurate, and more and more detailed. It is hard work, though, you have to practise, and practise, and practise. And you have first to be alone when you are doing it, otherwise, if there are people about chattering like a load of monkeys, they will distract you and you will never do it. So, practise, and practise alone until you are proficient. And when you are proficient you can do it with your hands or your feet, or you can even sit on a letter and know what's inside!

Still dealing with Mrs. Sorock, we have her final questions, 'How can one make sure lessons are learned well enough so we don't have to come and start all over again?'

Believe me that when you get a lesson which you FEEL has sunk in, it has indeed sunk in. You want to remember that when you leave this world you leave all your money behind you, you leave your clothes behind you, and this low-vibration physical body as well. But what actually goes with you in place of a bank account is all the good that you ever learned. So if you have had a lesson or two, that goes with you, and you have the results of that on the Other Side. Supposing you are having difficulty with some man; you decide on a certain course of action to 'bring him to heel', and then you weaken when the time comes for you to implement that course of action. Well, that sets up a negative, it sets up a black mark against you. If you have decided to do a certain thing which you believe to be right, then you must at all costs do that thing which you believe to be right. If you start to do it, and turn back, then it acts as a negative, it acts as a barrier, and as some great difficulty which later has to be overcome.

To answer your question, then—how to make sure that you learn your lessons well enough so that you do not have to come here again. Decide upon what you believe is a correct course of action, and having decided upon that correct course of action, let nothing divert you from your course. Then you will be doing right, and you will not have to come and learn it all over again.

You can also practise the old immortal law—'Do as you would be done by.' If you do that, then you have learned the great law of all, and you do not have to come back and start all over again.

So, let us say goodbye to Mrs. Valeria Sorock on these questions, and turn to something else, shall we?

Questions, questions, questions! All right—what

is the next question?

'You write in your books about two Siamese cats, one called Ku'ei and one called Fifi. What happened to them?'

The Lady Ku'ei is not upon this Earth any more. She was doing very well, but then I was the victim of a wholly unjustified, entirely unwarranted press attack and the Lady Ku'ei, who, like me, had had a very hard life, was not able to put up with any more sorrow or persecution. And so the Lady Ku'ei passed away from this Earth. I visit her in the astral and she visits me. Mrs. Fifi Greywhiskers also has left this Earth, but she was old and blind. She was gravely handicapped by the beastliness of humans. She is now handicapped no longer, for she can see. And she has a very, very sweet nature; I visit her, too, in the astral and she visits me. These two have their 'representatives' here, one is Miss Cleopatra, a seal point Siamese, and I must say that she is the most intelligent animal I have ever met. If one were awarding I.Q.'s one would place her I.Q. rating very, very high indeed. She is brilliant. The other 'representative' is Miss Tadalinka, and she is a blue point Siamese. She is exceptionally kind-hearted and most maternal. She comes into my room at night and really looks after me, and they both are the finest of all companions during the long, sleepless hours of darkness.

Never let anyone say that humans are superior to animals, for these two—Cleopatra and Tadalinka—have personalities which, in a human, would raise them to sainthood, and that is truly meant.

Another person writes, 'In one of your books you imply that the Christian religion is breaking down, and there will be trouble in the Vatican in years to come. Don't you think the Christian religion will conquer all?'

Actually, it's not what I think; that doesn't matter. What DOES matter is, what is present in the Akashic

Probabilities. And according to the Akashic Record of Probabilities, the Christian religion will pass away. Already Christians (I am a Buddhist!) are saying that God is dead, or God doesn't care, or some such rot. But God is God no matter what you call Him. There is a Supreme Being no matter what you call Him.

A great weakness of Christianity is that Protestant fights against Catholic, and Catholic fights against everything else, and they are all so frightfully sure that there is no way to Heaven except through the door of their own particular little Church. The Record of Probabilities says that before too long the Christian religion will end and a completely fresh religion will come into being. Many people believe that there are more Christians than any other religion upon this Earth. That is nonsense which can be shown by visiting any Public Library and consulting a map which gives comparative religious numbers.

The Christian religion will end, then, and a completely fresh religion will take its place in which some of the priests, most of the priests, will have a far greater understanding of people than do the present Christian priests, who are scared stiff to discuss anything and who can only talk in platitudes or parables. It's easy for a priest, with an absolutely assured income, to prate on to some poor impoverished sufferer about, 'God will provide.' But it's not so easy when you are the poor impoverished sufferer. With the next religion there will be many, many improvements. About time, too, isn't it?

In passing, and this is entirely my own comment, I really am highly amused about the Salvation Army; these people used to be wonderful to the poor, but my own personal experience is that they are not so wonderful now. Now you get little men and women who, to me, seem to be arrant hypocrites lording it over those who have had some misfortunes. I am not speaking from hearsay for I have had misfortunes, I know what it's like to be forced to live for a short time in a Salvation Army hostel and to have a little squirt of a man order me about. I know what it's like to have a little runt squeal, 'Sing, my man, you have to sing and pray before you have your soup.' Let me repeat that many years ago the Salvation Army did wonderful things for the poor, but during the last twenty-five years they seem to have changed such a lot that it's about time they were disbanded and set to digging ditches, or something, so they would know the other side of the coin. That is my personal opinion based upon more than one actual personal, painful, experience of the Salvation Army.

Reference to an army of any kind, good, bad, or very indifferent, brings our next question into its logical position. A questioner wrote, 'What is wrong with this world? Why have we failed, where have we failed? How is it that everyone's hand is against everyone else nowadays? Can you explain that?'

Yes, I think so. I think there is no problem in explaining actually. It's a breakdown in discipline. An army is only an army so long as it has discipline. When discipline fails an army becomes a rabble. But, let us look at it rather more closely.

Every person, every community, whether it be a hamlet, a village, a town, a city, or a country, and every world also, has a choice of the right Path or the wrong Path. It's like a continuous examination. Do people know the answers? Can they make the right decision, the right choice? Can they take the right Path?

Well, the poor old Earth took the wrong Path, and what could have been the negation of the Age of Kali in which all the horrors, frustrations, etc., of the Age of Kali would have been cancelled out, instead of that the Earth took the wrong Path and the Age of Kali is upon us in full force.

This is how it started. In 1914 World War 1 began.

Men were sent to the fighting forces and because of avaricious munition makers and others of that ilk, women were beguiled into cutting their hair short, putting on trousers and entering the factories, taking over the jobs formerly held by men. Women went to work, women sought what they blithely called 'equality with men'. And what utter nonsense that is! Men and women are different; no man has ever produced a baby, and no woman has ever fathered a baby. They are quite different. Each designed for their own purposes in life, in evolution. The job of the woman was probably far more important than that of men, women had equality, women have always had equality. The supreme job of women was to look after the family and to train the children to be good citizens and good people. When the woman was at home looking after the family the world was a far better place, there were less crimes, less strikes, less civic disturbances. Women stayed at home, maintained home discipline, and saw that the rising generation had the necessary training and the necessary discipline with which they, in turn, would take over.

But then women entered the factories, entered the shops, they drove buses, did everything. And what happened? Young children were shoved out into the streets to play, to look after themselves. Young children, almost as soon as they could totter, were left to fend for themselves and go to a drug store for a hurriedly snatched meal. The weaker characters among these young people, these quite young children, were soon dominated by stronger and harder and more vicious characters in the community. Soon children were racing about in gangs like pack rats. There is no longer a respect for law and order. A policeman is an object of derision. Everything is done by children to break the law, they lie, they steal, they gamble, and their sexual precociousness makes one wonder what is to happen next.

Parents no longer have any real authority over their children. Children stay out at all hours of the day and night, they are not responsible to anyone. These children flaunt the authority of teachers, and they behave like mad things. They grow up to be gangsters and assassins, and, in my considered opinion, the whole responsibility is that of parents who are so busy amassing money that it is an economic necessity that husband and wife both work, and thus the children, the future race, are neglected. As husband and wife both work there is more money available, so manufacturers put on extra shifts of workers to make more goods, to take some of the surplus money. The goods are carefully made so that they last a certain predictable time only, or utterly lying advertisements preach that it is absolutely necessary to have this or that product to be 'in'. Cars are altered year after year in only their tinny details; they are altered to make last year's cars completely obsolete fashionwise. Yet underneath there is the same old clonker rattling along, the same old engine which really hasn't improved much over the years. All that matters to people now is—are they keeping up with the Joneses? Better—can they go one step ahead of the Joneses?

The world has gone mad, and it's all because men and women want to take a country and 'squeeze it like a lemon'. Here in Canada a member of the Mail Carriers Union, or whatever they call themselves, who have gone on strike causing distress and hardship for many because they want a thirty per cent increase in their already lavish wages, has gone on the radio and actually broadcast (in by no means cultured tones!) that the country is like a lemon and the Unions are going to squeeze the last drop of juice out. Well, as long as that attitude prevails the country, and the world, has little hope.

The only thing to save the world now is a return to sanity, a return to the realisation that the man should be earning the living and the woman should be the mother, the woman should stay at home doing the most noble task of all, instilling discipline and spiritual values into children who later will become adults and so in their turn will have to pass on knowledge and training. The world lacks religion. So many religions are busy fighting against each other. The Christian, for example—well, it should be that Christianity is Christianity. Instead, the Church of England and the Church of Rome hail it as a great spiritual victory when they can speak politely to each other. They are all Christians, aren't they? What is wrong with them, why do they treat members of any other sect as criminals, as people bound for Hell? What does it matter if a person is a Jew, a Christian, a Buddhist, or a Hindu? They all believe in their own form of religion, don't they? And as such their own form of religion should be respected. It seems that the Catholic world is much the same as Communism; the Communists try to inflict their belief on everyone regardless of the other person's wishes. The Catholics, also, try to force their religion down another person's throat and they utter direful threats of eternal torment, eternal damnation, and all that rot. Believe me when I say that there is no such thing as Hell, believe me when I say that all roads lead the same way Home. You have to die whatever your religion. You will die if you have no religion just the same as the Pope himself. And all that matters is, have you lived your life according to your own personal belief? You won't find a fat priest ready to answer for your sins after. He won't take the blame for anything. You are strictly on your own. What you do and what you do not is not your own responsibility entirely, and you answer to yourself only, not to an avenging judge who is going to sentence you to an eternity in Hell. No! There is nothing like that.

You criticise yourself, and, believe me, there is no harsher critic of your actions than yourself.

But everyone gets a chance, and a fresh chance, and another chance after that. This is getting away from our subject, however.

We need spiritual discipline. A religion is a useful thing for inculcating spiritual discipline provided the religious leaders are not fighting among themselves. All the present day religions fall down on the job, and so all the present Earth religions shall, before too long, pass away like shadows disappearing in the night, and a fresh religion shall come to this Earth which shall help lift people out of the darkness and the misery into which they have now sunk.

But the time is not yet. The Final Battle is not yet. First there is more suffering, more disturbances in this, the Age of Kali, disturbances caused by World War 1 in which women deserted their homes and their children and left those children to run wild on the streets. If you get a wonderfully kept orchard, an orchard on which great care and endless expense has been lavished, and you suddenly withdraw all care from that orchard, everything soon becomes third-rate. The fruit no longer has the bloom and the fullness of constant care, instead that fruit becomes wrinkled and bitter. People are getting like that. People are now of inferior stock, and soon there will have to be the leaving process again so that fresh blood is brought to the Earth.

But first there will be more suffering. First the whole world will be engulfed by a form of Communism. Not the Communism of China where even clocks and cars are supposed to run by the illustrious thoughts of Chairman Mao Tse Tung, and where, apparently, if a person has some interior obstruction he just thinks of old Mao Tse Tung, and there is such a disturbance that everything is cleared away immediately!

So Earth is in for a sickener, Earth is in for a bad time, let's face it frankly. Everything is going to be engulfed in this form of Communism. Everyone will be given a number, they might even lose their names and identities. All these strikes are going to price things out of existence. The Unions are gaining more and more power, and eventually they will take over with the private armies of sheep-like workers, and that will be a major step towards the ruination of the Earth. Eventually the press lords, like the robber barons of old, will mobilise their private armies of press workers and they will go to even lower depths in their attacks on people, attacks which are so difficult to stand against when even the meanest type of reporter can write things in the columns of his paper and the attacked person has no redress whatever. This isn't justice. This isn't fair. And it's this type of sub-human person who is ruling the Earth today and will bring the Earth down even lower and lower. Until, having unnecessarily touched rock-bottom in this, the Age of Kali, the indomitable spirit existing in some people will shudder with the shock and the shame of what has fallen upon the Earth, and the spirit will revolt and will take action which will enable Earth and the peoples of Earth to rise again. But it may be necessary for the peoples of space, the Gardeners of Earth, to come and give assistance.

This is the Age of Assassination. A great religious leader, Martin Luther King, was assassinated. He was a good man and had much to give to this Earth. As for the others, well—they were just political people and (I do not want to tread on anyone's toes!) history will prove that these were dwarfs raised to giant stature only by the appalling power of their advertising machine, an advertising machine which blew out a lot of stinking hot air and made dwarfs appear like giants, just as you can get a toy soldier and by placing a light behind him you can make his shadow giant-size on the wall behind. But here, too, the toy soldier's shadow is a shadow only, something without substance, something that soon will be forgotten. Martin Luther King was no shadow. He was a good man, working for the good, not only of coloured people but of people of all colours throughout the world. For, in persecuting blacks, or browns, or reds, or yellows, the white people who are doing the persecuting are placing a terrible amount of Kharma upon themselves individually and collectively, and whatever they are doing now to the coloured people will have to be atoned for in suffering and toil and humility.

There would still be time to save this Earth from its degradation, from its shame, if only women would return to their homes and look after the children and see that those children had proper training, because it is the lack of training which makes it possible for assassins to go about their filthy work. It is the lack of training which enables race riots to take place, and looting, and rape. These things were not common in the days when women had more than equality at home; when she occupied the supreme place of honour as Mother to her family.

It would be much, much better if the criterion of womanhood could be: How well behaved are her children? How contented is her husband? How useful is this woman to the community? Is she an example to others? If so she is a woman to be proud of. Now, sad to say, a woman is judged by her mammary development, whether they stick up or down, how accessible they are, and how many husbands she has had. Sex is a wonderful thing, but this isn't sex. The people who go in for this type of thing are immature. They don't know anything about LOVE, but only about the most functional aspects of procreation, and then, interestingly enough, most of these sex queens are as impotent as a eunuch who has been treated twice by mistake!

If all of us could issue a prayer that a Great Leader would come to Earth and help to straighten out the mess, that Great Leader would come, not with flaming sword and embattled hosts because wars never settle anything, wars just make misery, wars make more troubles. It's not necessary to have any of those things. The way of peace is the best, and the best way to get peace is to get women back in the homes teaching decency to the male members of the family. They can do it, you know. Remember the old saying? 'A woman who is good is very good, but a woman who is bad is worse than any man could ever be no matter how bad.'

CHAPTER SIX

A PALE sun shone wanly down through a widening gap in the slowly dispersing clouds. The mountain heads were invisible, hidden in white fleecy softness which billowed, cleared, and descended again as if reluctant to loosen its all-enshrouding grasp of the steep mountain-sides.

Below, the Valley of Lhasa was gleaming, newly-washed by the recent torrential downpour. Innumerable frogs sat on the banks of the lake, croaking away in thankfulness for the flood of insects who had been washed from the leaves of distant trees, and then fallen, willy-nilly, into the ever-waiting mouths below.

The willows sighed and rustled gently as the raindrops trickled down from the topmost leaves, and then sank with soft musical 'plops' into the waters of the lake. The golden roofs of the Potala gleamed whitely under the subdued sunlight, and from the City of Lhasa there sprang a rainbow which began at the Jo Kang Cathedral, and arced all the way up into the clouds.

The formerly deserted Linghor Road—the Ring Road—was now filling up with people again. They had vanished into any available shelter when the rains came teeming down, almost drowning the countryside and swelling the river, making it almost burst its banks. Even now, great torrents of water were rushing down the mountain-sides and slowly the level of the lakes and the marshes crept up. With little gurgling moans land which had been dry, and even parched, for weeks past now greedily absorbed the unexpected supply of rain water.

On the Happy River the boatman, astride his inflated skin ferry, was looking anxiously at the sky, worrying lest fresh torrents of rain should make it impossible for him to cross the river. For a skin boat leaves much to be desired in the way of safety, and it is so easy to slide off and plummet into the water. Ferrymen, like sailors the world over, rarely know how to swim, and this ferryman had no conception of that art.

But the Road was filling up again. Household monks going about their task of getting supplies from the Market Place of Lhasa. Water-bearing monks scampering down the rocky path to the little well, now overflowing, and then trudging slowly, tiredly up that path again carrying the essential water, for the Potala and for Chakpori too, for Chakpori, although much smaller in population, used for its size a vast amount of water because of the preparations of herbs and other forms of medical treatment.

On the Road lamas went about their business. High Lamas with their retinue of waiting-monks, and others who disdained the trappings of rank, rode on in solitary splendour or with just one attendant following. Traders, with grunting yaks, made their slow way through the Western Gate and on the last stage of their journey to Lhasa. Traders avid for profit, but avid for talk. Avid, too, for the open-mouthed wonderment with which some of their stories would be heard!

From the other direction, from the City itself, other traders were setting out, setting out to climb the mountain passes and to make their slow way through snow-laden rock surfaces where a slip would mean death, and then, the dangers surmounted, they would eventually, in days or weeks, reach India, reach Kalimpong, and other trade centres. About to pass each other, arriving traders and departing traders, would exchange a shouted conversation, giving the state of the market, the latest news, the disposition of the people.

By the side of the Pargo Kaling, beggars sat, moaning and calling for alms. Calling for all the blessings possible on those who gave, and all the maledictions imaginable on those who refused to give. Tourists and pilgrims thronged the road, going right round the Potala, and circling the lake and the great rock in which were carved religious figures, and which were kept gaily coloured. Pilgrims and tourists, the doves, and among them the hawks—those who preyed upon the pilgrim and the tourist, those who sold horoscopes saying that each horoscope was personally prepared under the direction of a High Lama. And all the time those horoscopes had been bought in bulk, after having been printed in India.

Here, perched upon a convenient rock, stood an old man, calling forth to the tourists, 'Look at this, look at this!' he quoth, 'Talismans and charms which have been personally seen and blessed by the Inmost One. This will save you from the Devils which afflict, this will save you from the illnesses which lay one low.'

He looked about, eager to spot a gullible person who would fall for that line of talk. A little distance away a woman stood, whispering to her husband, 'Blessed by the Inmost One!' she whispered. 'That must indeed command a high price,' said the husband. 'But we must have it! I am with child and we need a good Talisman now to make sure that our child is born under happy auspices.'

Together, they moved towards the Seller of Talismans who, seeing their eagerness, moved towards them, and as they met he drew them to one side, to a little grove of willows, so that he could discuss the price and get all that 'the market would bear'. Having made their purchase, the husband and wife walked away hand in hand, smiling contentedly, thinking that now they had protection bestowed by the blessing of the Inmost One of the very sacred Talisman. And the Seller of Talismans? He hurried away to take up his post again, and tell the old, old tale of the Talismans and the Charms that would bring good luck.

'Tell me,' said the letter, 'where can I get a really good Talisman that will bring me good fortune and protect me from ill? I have seen many advertisements in the So-and-So Magazine, but I do not know what I should buy.'

Well, the best thing is to buy none. None of these Talismans or Charms are worth anything at all.

Now, let us be reasonable about this; if things are just mass-produced, stamped out by the thousands, probably untouched by human hand, they can have no effect at all. When, in the Lamaseries, I was taught that the only way to make a good Talisman or a good Charm was to make it personally, and imbue it with a personality, or thought-entity. I state emphatically that any commercially made charm or talisman is just a waste of money.

Let me tell you a simple little story: Some time ago I received a small packet from a man in the U.S.A. He wrote to me as well, and said that he had sent me a piece of bark from a very special tree in Ireland. He said it was guaranteed to bring Good Luck and protect me from evil.

The piece of bark came to me in a special envelope, and there was a folder with it. There was also the picture of a small tree. The folder went on to say that for over three hundred years pieces of bark had been cut from this tree, and had been sold all over the world. Wherever there were people, said the folder, these pieces of bark had been sent. Thousands of pieces, millions of pieces.

Now, I ask you, what sort of tree can supply bark for three hundred years and not die? What sort of tree can supply millions of pieces of bark, and keep on healing and growing? I turned the thing over in my hands, and by psychometry I came to the inescapable conclusion that someone was 'pulling a fast one' by buying up bark from trees which had been felled, and with a punch cutting out pieces about the size of a half dollar, and sending them all over the world. The profit must have been truly enormous. 'What a pity,' I thought, 'that I am an honest man. That's the way to raise money for research!' But, sadly enough, honesty prevails, and it always will in the end, you know!

There is no 'virtue' in charms or talismans which have been mass-produced, either by stamping out of metal, or casting in metal, or printing. They are quite useless. The only talismans or charms which have any use whatever are those which have actually been made, and a thought-form built into each individual charm. It can be done, and it is done. But it cannot be done on a commercial basis because the time alone would make a charge of a couple of hundred dollars utterly necessary.

Perhaps I should explain here that Rampa Touch-Stones are a different thing altogether. They are not charms, they are not talismans. They are special devices which are used by one owner, and which quickly generate great force, and which help that one owner. They cannot be used by two people, and, as thousands of letters testify, they really DO work. But—they are not talismans, they are not charms; they are something absolutely different.

This and That Magazine have all these advertisements about the Star of This, or the Star of That, or the Circle of Something Else. Well, I suppose people have to live, and they should remember—'*Caveat emptor*'—which means, of course, 'Let the buyer beware'. Magazines make their income from advertising, and I assume that the Advertising Editor of a magazine reads the advertisements with his eyes shut if there is any possibility that they won't really be suitable. Remember, then, that if you go and buy a talisman or charm—well, you have done some good to someone, possibly, in turning over some good money for a bad object.

It really is a fact, however, that if one wants a talisman or charm—call it what you will—it can be made if you know how, if you have the time, the patience, and the determination. You do not get it made overnight. It takes time, the time depending upon the effect you want.

You will have heard of curses put on old Egyptian tombs, or certain artefacts of antiquity which have a spell or curse upon them. These things are real, they are not just imagination. What happened was that people who knew how to set about it made a thought-form, and 'magnetised it' to the object to be protected. The thought-form comes into action when certain conditions are present. That is, if a person is trying to steal the artefact, thoughts are emanated from the would-be thief, and those thoughts trigger the pre-conditioned automatic response of the thought-form. So the would-be thief drops dead of apparent heart failure, or something like that.

It is a long and complicated process, and one which cannot be duplicated by mass-production methods. From which it is very obvious that a lot of those silly little charms which are advertised are not worth buying unless you want them for a talking point.

Now there is an interesting question: 'Since living in an apartment building I have not been so well. An old country woman told me that it was because I lived off the ground. Is that really true?'

Yes, it is! It is very, very true. Let's look at the problem, shall we?

The Earth, in one sense, is a magnet. It is a ball which contains magnetic forces of varying degrees of intensity. Anyone knows that there is a North Pole and a South Pole. People are taught that from earliest schooldays. But not so many know that continental masses and islands, and, in fact, everywhere, have their own particular amount of magnetism. It is easily measured that gravity—a form of magnetism— is different in various parts of the world, and it is constantly measured that magnetism is different everywhere. Ships' compasses, for example, can read differently in the varying ports throughout the world, and on many coastlines one can see two white cones, usually of pyramid shape, and so sited that when viewed from a certain distance and a certain position at sea they form just one apparently solid bar of white. Ships manoeuvre in a port to line themselves up with these two markers, and when an imaginary centre line, drawn from the stern through the bows, exactly meets the two white markers, which now appear as one, then the compass aboard the ship should read a certain heading. If it does not, small adjusting magnets are put in a box beneath the compass to pull or push the compass card to the desired position.

This 'adjusting the compass' is also carried out on aircraft. Admitted, a compass may be affected by the nature of the cargo of a ship, but even when that is compensated for the magnetic variation of different land masses must also be taken into account.

The different intensities of magnetism affect people. People have a lot of iron in them, as well as other minerals and chemicals, and a person living in an area of high magnetic density will react differently in his thoughts from a person who lives in a low density magnetic area.

You can say that Germans and—who shall we say?—Argentinians are quite different in their make-ups, in their reactions, and quite a lot of that is due to the magnetic pull exerted upon the German in Germany, and the Argentinian in Argentina. The nature of the food eaten and the amount of iron intake also should be taken into account. And, whereas a German could live in apartment buildings without any really serious health effects, the average Argentinian citizen would feel crushed and depressed in similar conditions because the magnetism, or rather, the degree of magnetism, in Argentina makes for a free type of people who will not be regimented so much as the Germans in Germany. Observe that I say 'Germans in Germany'. That is to indicate that when a German leaves Germany or an Argentinian leaves Argentina, they come more under the influence of the magnetism of the country in which they will then be residing.

Anything is affected by the basic magnetism of the country. Every creature of Earth needs to be in contact with the Earth currents. The Earth currents, of course, are the particular degree of magnetism in that area. If a person is denied access to contact with the Earth, his health deteriorates. Recent studies have proved most conclusively that people who live in apartment buildings, and who have little access to a garden or park where there is natural, unpaved ground, suffer from nerve conditions and generally poor health. Everyone knows that the people who live in the country are stronger and in better health than those who live in the city.

In the country a person can go out and walk in the fields, can get in contact with good, clean water. Whereas, in the cities, everything is paved over with a mixture of tar and stone or artificial stone, materials which tend to insulate the human body from the Earth's currents.

In certain languages there are stories of giants who went to war and who were on the point of being defeated in battle. The giants then lay down on the ground for a few moments, and jumped to their feet as 'giants refreshed'. In other words, they picked up energy from the Earth currents, and by lying down to pick up that energy they pulled a fast one over their enemies!

Everyone who desires good health should be able to get out in the country, and be able to take off their shoes and stockings and walk about on the good, cool earth. If people did that there would be less illness, less frustration, less tension.

While on this subject of Earth currents, one might mention the position in which one should sleep. Now, people are not rubber stamp impressions. Not all people are alike. But all people can benefit to an astonishing degree by sleeping in such a position that they derive the maximum gain from the natural Earth currents.

The best way to do this is to set aside a month for experiment. For one week have your bed facing North, and make a careful day by day note of how you slept and how you feel with the bed facing North. For the next week have the bed facing, say, East, and again make careful notes of how you feel. With following weeks, try sleeping with your head to South, and then to West. At the end of a month you will have a very good idea of which direction suits you, and if you then move your bed permanently to that position you will find that 'fortune' will smile upon you, and you will feel better in health. If you have been using a double bed—well, you will either have to be counted out of this experiment, or you will have to have a single bed.

It used to be thought that being in contact with the sea had the same type of effect upon humans, but that is not really so. People feel better when they are in contact with the sea because usually the air is better and more healthful. But the magnetic currents of the sea are quite different from the magnetic currents of the land, and while it does no harm to go and 'dunk' yourself in the sea, do it for pleasure only, and not with the particular intention of deriving health benefits from sea magnetic currents. You may get some benefit from getting a good salt solution around your pores, and you will get a lot of benefit from the fresher air which usually blows over the sea. But then, you might get a load of dirty oil from some filthy oil ship, or, as where I live now, foul effluvia and floating debris from a pulp mill which discharges all its waste into the river, and so it flows on past my window into the sea, with a stench which is truly an abomination.

Another person writes in—'How are we only one-tenth conscious? If we are only one-tenth conscious, how do we manage to paddle around as we do?'

The answer is that we just ARE one-tenth conscious. After all, you can have a car and you can move around at ten miles an hour. You can even have a thing fitted to limit your speed to a predetermined amount, and then, although the car is capable of much more speed, you are limited to that to which the car has been preconditioned. The human limit is one-tenth conscious. If one could get one-and-one-half-tenth conscious, then one would have a genius, but all too often if a person is super-bright in one direction he glows remarkably dimly in some other direction. Such as a man who is a brilliant inventor, an absolutely superb brain in, let us say, electronics, and yet in other ways he is so stupid that he has to be led around, and dressed, and fed, etc. I know such a case.

The one-tenth consciousness is something like a telephone operator who sits at a switchboard with ten telephone lines in front of her. She can only deal with one at a time, so she is dealing with a tenth. Humans are nine-tenths sub-conscious. 'Sub' because it is beyond our conscious reach, it is beneath our consciousness. The Overself is above our consciousness, and the consciousness can be likened to the amount of an iceberg which shows above water. Only a little of an iceberg shows above water, the great mass of it lies submerged beneath the surface, in just the same way as the great mass of human knowledge lies submerged just beneath the threshold of consciousness. Hence the name 'sub-conscious'.

Under certain conditions the sub-conscious can be tapped. It is possible by the appropriate processes to get in touch with the sub-conscious and find out what it knows, and what it knows is this; it knows everything that has ever happened to that entity. 'That entity', please, not just that particular human body! By really getting down to the sub-conscious one engages in a process like getting down into the basement of some great Library or some great Museum, and seeing the vast array of things which are stored but which are not on show. Museums, you know, have more things concealed than they have displayed.

Tap the sub-conscious of a human, and you can find out all about anything that has ever happened to that human. You can follow the life in reverse. You can take the person now aged, let us say, seventy years, and you can take them back sixty, fifty, forty, and so on right back to the moment of birth, right back to the moment when that person was born to this Earth. And if you then change technique, like a car changing gear, you can follow the sub-conscious beyond birth, you can find the moment when the entity actually entered the body of the unborn baby. You can find out what the entity did before it entered the body of the unborn baby. And if your reason is sufficiently good, you can find out what that person was in the past life, or the life before that, or the life before that, and that, and so on.

A warning; do not believe all the advertisements which claim that Madame Dogsbody will do all this for you for a fee of one dollar. These things cannot be done for money, they cannot be done for idle curiosity. It needs a lifetime of study and a serious purpose. It is not a circus turn. So—don't waste your money!

I am one of those who can do this. I can do it for myself, also, and I know a surprising amount about myself, going back, and back, and back.

But let me issue another warning; don't believe all these people who wear a shawl around their heads or say they will visit the Akashic Record for a few dollars, or a few hundred dollars, and come back with all the knowledge. If they could do this, they would not be doing it for money, they would know better. But if you pay your money down, they will 'come back' with suitable histrionic effects and tell you that you were Cleopatra or Napoleon or Old Kaiser Bill or Castro's grandfather, or even de Gaulle's uncle. They usually try to find out who you would like to be, and then they 'come back' with a great shaking of head, and a great pursing of lips, and all the other effects, and tell you all that you have told them—but they are careful to use different words. No, madam! The world is over-stocked with those who have been Cleopatra. No, sir! The world is over-stocked with those who have been St. Peter or St. John, or St. Somebody Else. And anyhow, what does it matter who you were? You were someone, quite definitely, but what does it matter? You now have a different name, you now have a different body, you now have a different task in life and it doesn't do to dwell on past glories. The past does not matter. The past has made the failures of the present. All you can do now is to live a decent life in the present to make a better future.

The best way is to avoid going to fortune tellers

and avoid dealing with those who advertise that they will do this, that, and something else if you pay them enough. If you want to know about yourself, and you have sufficient reason, you can always do it by astral travel. If you want to know something, then try meditation. There is a chapter about it in *Chapters of Life*.

In meditation you have to insulate yourself against Earth currents, because if you have Earth currents circulating around, then you think about Earth things, you think 'Earth-wise'. And you don't want to do that, you want to be able to control the subject of your meditation. So the first requisite for meditation is that you avoid our old friend constipation (oh! it's a very important subject!), and you put on a meditation robe. This is nearly always of black material, and it must cover you from head to foot. It must actually cover your head, and cover most of your face. You don't have to suffocate yourself, of course, and if your meditation robe is properly designed you won't. But the whole point is that you have to be insulated by this black cloth from outside influences. Your body must be protected from sunlight, because sunlight will colour your thoughts, and you don't want your thoughts coloured. You want to think your own thoughts, and have your own thoughts under your own control.

If you look in *Chapters of Life* you will find a picture of a monk. Well, if you are handy with a needle and thread, make up a thing like that, but be sure it's big enough. It doesn't matter if it's like a tent, or like a sack; you are not going to be a fashion model in it, that's not its purpose. Its whole and only purpose is to cut off external influences, so the fit doesn't matter and the larger it is—within reason, of course—the more comfortable it will be. You should keep this meditation robe for meditation alone, and you should not wear it for any other purpose than when you are meditating. You should also keep it safely away so that no one else can use it, and no one else can touch it, because if another person touches it and tries it on, you have that other person's influence in the robe—which you are trying to avoid—and so you have another obstacle.

By meditating under this insulated, isolated condition, you are immune to outside influences. Thus, you can get really down to the heart of the matter in which you are interested. You can take yourself through the various stages of meditation, going deeper and deeper and deeper, so that in the end you can be meditating in such a state that you are floating. And when you have reached that stage you can know quite a lot about what goes on beyond the tenth. Beyond the tenth of consciousness, and into the ninetenths of sub-consciousness. Remember again, though, that this 'sub-conscious' does not mean that this particular phase of consciousness is inferior. The word 'sub' usually means 'inferior', but in this sense it is taken to indicate that which is below the threshold of consciousness, whereas supra would indicate that which is beyond, or above, the threshold of consciousness.

So the sub-conscious relates to everything that a person knows or has known, or has experienced at any time since that person first became an entity. Taking the present as our datum line, we can say that all that is past, or all that is stored, is 'below'. Whereas, all that which is to come and which has yet to be experienced on this Earth or in the next world, is in the 'supra-consciousness', which is, therefore, above our datum line.

All right! So now you know a bit more about our title of *Beyond the Tenth*. We deal with, and have dealt with things which people know without knowing why, and the things which people can do although, for the present perhaps, they think they cannot. To wit—astral travel. Anyone can do it! Anyone can do it with a bit of patience and adherence to a few simple rules, but people say, 'oh, I couldn't possibly do that!' Really, they are afraid to make the attempt, but you—dear Reader—make the attempt, because it truly is a wonderful, wonderful experience to be soaring and sailing above the surface of the Earth, playing with the wind, causing birds, who can see the astrals of people, to fairly shriek with amazement. You try it. You'll find it's the most wonderful thing that has ever happened to you.

Of course there is far more to this soaring above the Earth business than just play. One can go to any part of the world, as I have already told you, but that is not the extent of it; there is more—much more—than this.

If one meditates, if one becomes really proficient at meditation, and one combines that with astral travel, one is not limited to the face of the Earth. Keep this in mind; when doing astral travel we are not in a flesh body, we are in a body which can penetrate materials which, to the flesh body, would be solid. Do you understand the implications of that? It means that one can sink downwards at a controlled rate, sink down through the Earth and through solid rock. One can see with perfect clarity, although to a flesh body it would be complete and utter darkness. One can sink down and see perhaps here a giant figure which was trapped half a million years ago and became embedded in what is now solid coal. In this solid coal, then, there is a giant figure intact, perfectly preserved, as mastodons and dinosaurs have been preserved intact.

For years scientists have thought that the advent of humans, or humanoid races, on the Earth was fairly recent. But they have now come to the conclusion that humanity on Earth is much, much older than previously thought. Our travels through solid rock can tell us that, our travels can indicate to us this; after thousands and thousands of years the Earth goes into a sort of periodic convulsion during which the whole surface of the Earth trembles, during which waters recede here and waters rise there. The surface of the Earth seems to boil and seethe, and every trace of the Works of Man upon the Earth rises up and falls down, and gets buried hundreds, or thousands, of feet below the surface of the Earth. Housewives will understand when I say it is similar to making a big cake; you have a basin full of all sorts of unmixed ingredients, and then you insert a big spoon from the bottom and raise up, gradually mixing everything so that all the components, all the constituents, are distributed throughout the cake mix.

So, every half million years, or so, the Earth gets rid of unwanted stock and prepares the surface of the Earth for the next bunch, who, it fondly hopes, might be more successful. Life on Earth is old, the Age of the dinosaur and the mastodon and all those creatures was just the start of yet one more experiment, just as in thousands of years to come, this Earth will end as we know it at present. The whole surface will seethe and bubble, and the cities and Works of Man here will tumble down, and be buried thousands of feet below the surface so that anyone coming to Earth would say it was a new world which had never been inhabited.

It takes a lot of experience to do this type of astral travel. But I can do it, and I can tell you that you can do it also if you will practise sufficiently, if you will have faith in your own ability, and if you will remember that you cannot do it to bring back messages for other people at so many dollars a visit!

I have seen deep down in the Arctic ice, hundreds of feet, or even thousands of feet below the surface, strange forms. A different form of human, a purplish type of person with different characteristics from present-day humans. Present-day humans have—just for example—two breasts and ten fingers. But I have seen purple people entombed absolutely intact, and they have had eight breasts and nine fingers on each hand. Probably some day research will exhume some of these people, and then there will be a nine-day wonder about it all. Some day there will be an atomic digging machine which will be able to excavate the ice, and show some of the people and some of the cities buried incredibly deep in the ice, cities of a people who lived and walked the surface of this Earth hundreds of centuries before there was any recorded history whatever on this Earth.

This was a time when there was only one continent on the Earth, and all the rest was water. When South America and Africa were one, and when England was just a part of mainland Europe; when Ireland was just a mountain peak stretching miles—yes, miles—up into the very different air. At one time all the world of land was one mass extending from the North Pole to what is now the South Pole. It was like a bridge linking one side of the Earth to the other. Australia, China, and America, all were one, all joined to what is now Africa and Europe. But in the earth-shakes, in the shivering tremors which threw down civilisation and threw up fresh earth and rocks to hide that civilisation, and because of centrifugal effects, that one solid mass, that one continent of Earth, broke up. And as the Earth shivered and trembled, the seabed crept along, taking bits of land with it, land which became Australia, America, Europe, Africa, and so on.

With practice in astral travel, with considerable practice in meditation, and combining the two together, you can actually see all this as if you were in that item beloved of the Science Fictioneer—a time machine. There really is a time machine, you know, a very definite, working, time machine; it is the

Akashic Record, wherein everything that has ever happened to this Earth is recorded. It's like having an endless number of cine cameras recording everything that ever happens, day or night, and blending them all together into one continuous ever-running film which you can 'tap into' by knowing how, and by knowing the age at which you desire to look.

It is truly a fascinating thing to see a civilisation upon the Earth, a flourishing civilisation, but one in which the people are very different from the humans whom we now are accustomed to see. In this particular civilisation, for example, people moved about not in motor cars, but on what may well be the origin of the old story about the flying carpet; they moved about on platforms which looked for all the world like mats. They sat cross-legged on these things and, by manipulating a little control which looked like a woven pattern, they could rise and soar off in any direction. In the Record we can watch all this, and then as we watch we have an effect just as if some clumsy person were shaking a chess board on which all the men were set up for a good game. As the chess-board men would tumble so did the people of the then-Earth tumble. The Earth itself yawned, great gaping chasms appeared, and buildings and people toppled in, and the Earth shuddered and closed up. And after a time the heaving and rolling of the surface ended, and the Earth was ready for the next 'crop'.

In this form of astral travel, also, one can go deep deep down into the Earth, and one can see perhaps intact afterfacts of that Age, or remnants of large buildings. One can go to Arctic or Antarctic regions, and go deep down and find people and animals who have been quick-frozen to death, and because of the cold and the quickness of the onset of the cold, they have been preserved utterly intact as if they merely slept and waited a shaking hand to awaken them.

As one looks one can see different chest developments, different nostrils, because the atmosphere of the Earth a few million years ago was very different from what it is today. People of today would not be able to live in the atmosphere of those times, just as people of those times would not have been able to breathe the atmosphere which we now optimistically call 'clean air'. Then there was far more chlorine, far more sulphur, in the air. Now we get the stink of petroleum fumes.

Another thing that you can see, and which you, like I, will no doubt find fascinating, is that petroleum is unnatural to this Earth. Petroleum is not native to this Earth. By the Akashic Record, a planet collided with this Earth and caused this Earth to stop for a moment, and then spin in the opposite direction. But the collision disintegrated the other planet, and much of its seas poured down through space on to this Earth. The seas of that planet were what we call petroleum. It poured down and saturated the Earth and sank into the Earth, and went on down until it found a level and a strata which it could not penetrate, and there it lay and collected, and awaited the coming of humans who would one day pump it up and invent a perfectly horrible machine or machines, which would use this petroleum. When all the petroleum has been used up there will be no more made, because, as I have said, it is just spillage from another world.

Have I said enough to really induce you to practise astral travel? It's a wonderful thing, and what we might term mundane (because it deals with the Earth) astral travel and meditation combined can show you all you could ever want to know about this Earth. So, why not try it? Why not have faith and patience, and really get down to practising astral travel?

CHAPTER SEVEN

Before I started to write this book I thought I would pay heed to all the thousands of letters which I had received demanding a book about herbal treatment. How could one cure this complaint, or alleviate that disease? I spent almost eighteen months trying to find a reputable firm, one in each in the main countries, who would supply the herbal treatment which I would recommend. I wrote to Messrs. Grassroots & Rissoles in England, telling them that I was going to write a book about herbal treatment and asking them if they could or would supply the herbs which I would recommend under the correct herbal name. I received a bland reply, which gave me politely to understand that they, and they only of anyone in the world, knew anything about herbs, and they were not prepared to depart from their system of calling a rose by another name, so to speak, by giving said rose a number!

I wrote to Toadstools and Applesauce Inc., of U.S.A., and asked them the same thing. The reply was delightfully evasive, and they said they would send me their latest catalogue giving the names of the particular concoctions which they put on the market. So I tossed their 'literature' in the trash can, and decided to write something else. The result is in this book so far, a book which is based wholly on answering the questions you ask about 'Beyond the Tenth'.

How can I, or anyone else, write a useful book

about herbal treatment when I cannot get a reliable supplier of those herbs? If I tell you that herb *XYZ* will cure you of whatever it is you are suffering from, then I am morally bound to tell you where to obtain herb *XYZ*. Unfortunately the herbal suppliers with whom I have been in contact merely want to say, 'Take our Pills Number 123 to cure your flatulence,' etc. That's not good enough for me. It's not good enough for you. You want to know what you are taking, you want to know what is in Pill 123. Certain herbs are very, very effective when taken in their pure or unadulterated form, but if one is going to put a cheaper type of herb in with it, then not only is the price cheaper, but the final product is unsatisfactory.

It seems the most astonishing thing—astounding would be a better word, perhaps—that suppliers of herbal treatment will not be straightforward and supply the actual herbs which one recommends, but instead want to give them some silly number or some fancy name like 'Eastern Cow's Breath'. I wrote to a small firm in England who were optimistically advertising Eastern herbs, but the good lady at the head of the firm hadn't the manners to reply to my letter. So that was another good idea lost. All I wanted was to make sure that you—my Readers—could have the assurance that if I recommended herb *XYZ* you could place an order and get herb *XYZ*. I did not want any commission or financial interest. I was thinking of my Readers only.

But, as I have said, I just cannot recommend a suitable source of supply, so for the herbs I am going to recommend in this chapter I advise you to consult your Classified Telephone Books and really shake up any herb supplier in your area. If I say a certain herb, then I mean that certain herb, I do not mean an adulterated substitute with a fragrant name or a number, and if the firm you contact first cannot supply you, try another firm perhaps in a different city.

Another difficulty is that what is a common herb in England is unknown in Canada, and what is an everyday sort of plant in Canada has never been heard of in the U.S.A. And what can you do in the Spanish world where they translate buttercup as poppy! In *Living with the Lama* I gave the name of 'Buttercup', yet in the Spanish editions the name was distorted to 'Poppy' because some of these Spanish countries are quite unaware of a buttercup.

It's all very strange, you know, that herbs have apparently fallen into disrepute. Nowadays the doctors and the chemists like to grub about with messy chemicals made of urea or some other noxious substance, whereas all they have to do is to go to the Brazilian forests where they can get just about any herb or plant in the world. Two hundred years ago a Doctor of Medicine in any European or English country had first to pass an examination in astrology, because astrology has great bearing on the effects of herbs, and then had to have a profound knowledge of the herbs themselves. He had to know how to erect a horoscope, and he had to know how and when herbs should be gathered.

One could see the Doctor of those days stealing out at night under the light of the moon, carefully consulting a chart in his hand to know exactly when a particular herb should be dug up or when certain leaves should be stripped from the branches.

In the Old School of Medicine astrology and herbs were absolutely inextricably entwined. Herbal treatment was 'sympathy and antipathy'. A disease caused by the bad effects of a particular planet could be cured by the use of herbs which were under the favourable influence of that same planet. They called that the Sympathetic Cure, and if you had ever tasted some of the herb teas they used you would agree that a great deal of sympathy was needed for the patient!

Again, a disease caused by a bad planet aspect could

be cured by a herb which was antipathetic to the planet causing the illness.

It used to be 'the thing' to look at the patient, to consider what his astrological influences would be, and frequently a horoscope was cast showing the malefic aspects upsetting the patient. Then the herb doctor would turn to his charts and books, and from his usually completely lavish stock he would produce herbs which would cure the illness within a matter of hours.

If one wants to do herbal treatment really effectively it has to be in conjunction with astrology, because every person—whether they believe it or not—has a make-up which is affected by astrological influences. If you want to be modern you will forget about astrological influences and call them 'cosmic rays', or something like that; but they are the same things—astrological influences. People who are born in the summer have a different chemical composition to people who are born in the winter, and what would have a strong effect upon the person born in the winter might have a mild effect only on the person born in the summer, and vice versa.

If we were going to set up as practitioners in herbal medicine, seeing our patients and all that, we would have to consider the astrological signs of each patient and the signs at the time he first noticed the illness, because humans have varying amounts of metal in them and they can be referred to as particles of different grades of iron differently affected by various magnets. The planets, of course, being the magnets.

Just to give you an idea about herbal treatment as confined to astrology, let me remind you that if a herb is under 'the domination' of the Sun it can cure illnesses of the Martian type of person. Mars people have their own peculiar illness, or rather, illnesses peculiar to Mars, just as Jupiter people have illnesses peculiar to Jupiter.

If a herb under the domination of **Venus** is used for Jupiter people, it will cure the illnesses peculiar to the Jupiter people, and herbs which are 'exalted' by Jupiter will cure those illnesses which may be termed 'Moon-type illnesses'. If you were really going into the subject you would say, 'Yes, that is because Jupiter reaches its exaltation in the sign of Cancer, which is the House of the Moon.'

You may be amused or interested to know that among the herbs ruled by the Moon are cabbage, cucumbers, cress, lettuce, pumpkin, watercress, and many others. But we are not going to study astrology, instead let us consider some common or garden illnesses about which a surprising number of people write to me. I am going to make very clear to you that if your condition is serious, then you should consult your family doctor—you know, the good old G.P.—and if your illness does not rapidly respond to any herbal treatment, then see your family doctor. On the other hand, if your family doctor has had an attempt at curing you and has not made the expected improvement, then try herbs; herbs were in existence long before the family doctors of the world!

It has just occurred to me that many of you throughout the world will not be able to get in touch with a local supplier of herbs, so I am going to give you two names and addresses, one in England and one in New York. If you write to these people they will only be able to supply their own mixtures or concoctions, but both firms are extremely reliable. Here they are:

Messrs. Heath & Heather Ltd.
St. Albans, Hertfordshire,
England

(*Special note:* The person to whom you should write is Miss Joan Ryder) and a convenience to you is that you can write in either English or Spanish, they understand both languages perfectly.

The second address is:

> Kiehl's Drugstore,
> 109 Third Avenue,
> New York 3, N.Y., U.S.A.

(*Special note:* The head man is Mr. Morse).

In both cases you should also remember to enclose ample return postage, because all these people are in business to make money, and as I very well know the cost of stationery and printing, the cost of having things typed, and then the final straw of the mail charge is just too much. You can send ample postage by International Reply Coupon; your post office will tell you about that. It is useless to write from America to England enclosing American postage, because American stamps are of no use whatever in England, just the same as English stamps cannot be used in the U.S.A. So, if you expect a reply, (and you must do or you wouldn't be writing in the first case!) remember the elementary courtesy of—(1) Providing ample return postage in the form of International Reply Coupons. (2) Put you full name and address on your letter, not merely on the back of the envelope. European customs are different, and in England it is the common practice to put the address of the sender at the top right-hand side of the letter itself, because English people toss out the envelope! (3) Do not get impatient if you do not get a reply by return because these firms are very busy firms, and, anyway, the ordinary transmission from country to country takes a certain amount of time.

When I am referring to a herb or treatment, then, I will confine myself to that which can be obtained from these two firms, and, of course, we will forget all about the astrological part!

One of the most common queries I get is: 'My husband is alcoholic. He is the kindest man alive when he is sober, but that is becoming more and more infrequent. I shall have to divorce him. What do you advise?'

It is a very sad, sad thing indeed that this business of drink has been allowed to continue. Drink definitely harms one's Overself, and if people did not drink they would not become alcoholic! The alcoholic state is not so much a vice as an illness, or dysfunction. What happens is that the blood of the alcoholic-type of person is defective, and it becomes very, very greatly harmed by the action of alcohol. Blood cells become changed, and a chemical change takes effect. A person who is alcoholic is a very, very sick person indeed, and no matter what anyone says, it is my experience that there is no cure for the alcoholic, no cure that is feasible. If a person is alcoholic he or she would have to be confined to a desert island in the hope that the blood might possibly become more normal in time.

If it was generally recognised that the alcoholic was a sick person with a blood disease, then doctors as a whole might give them some research attention. With adequate research there is every reason to suppose that a cure could be found for this truly distressing condition. The alcoholic drinks in order to live. He has a compelling urge to drink because he senses that there is something missing—and there is. His blood is different, and his blood can only be maintained by the continued application of alcohol to the blood-cells.

There are no herbs that can help the alcoholic. The only way that one can help the alcoholic is for him to enter a hospital, or other institution, where he can receive constant supervision and constant attention.

Often a person is born alcoholic-prone. That means

that one of the parents or one of the grandparents has been alcoholic, and so the person who is now born alcoholic-prone has a blood condition which could manifest itself after the intake of a certain amount of alcohol. It might be a thimbleful of alcohol that is required to trigger the reaction, or it might be a quart, no one knows. But when the reaction has been triggered there is no way of reversing it, and the person, instead of being alcoholic-prone, is instead a full-blown alcoholic.

It should be a law that alcoholics should register with a Medical Board. And then the children or grandchildren of an alcoholic parent or grandparent should be warned never to touch alcohol. As long as they don't touch the stuff they will, obviously, not become alcoholic. So, in this case, prevention is the only cure.

Alcoholics should not get married, and, as I have just stated, they should enter a hospital or institution so that they can be treated in accordance with any new developments which have been discovered. But let me say this in defence of the alcoholic; he is a sick man. Yes, he becomes vicious at times, he becomes uncaring, but he has a deadly illness, an insidious illness, and it won't help him at all to rant on at him, it will just drive him to desperation. Instead be firm with him, and tell him that his cure lies in his own hands by giving up alcohol. If he understands the problem, and if he has any will-power left, he can do much to alleviate the condition—for example, suck boiled sweets. That will help. So, that is the best I can tell you about how to treat alcoholics.

A surprising number of people write about asthma. Asthma can take various forms, and if a person has asthma he should go and see the doctor, see the General Practitioner, who will then, if necessary, refer the patient to a specialist. There is bronchial asthma, for example, and there are other forms of asthma, and they can be alleviated by the necessary medical or herbal treatment. I do not have Kiehl's catalogue here, but I can tell you that Heath & Heather have herbs for the relief of asthma, so there is no problem in connection with that.

For those who are interested, hyssop is a very good plant indeed for those afflicted with asthma. The best place from which to obtain the hyssop herb is Italy, because hyssop from Italy is more potent than from anywhere else. The Old People took hyssop which was boiled with a mixture of honey and rue, and then they drank the stuff. It gave instant relief from coughs and from shortness of breath and wheezing. Having taken the mixture I am not going to tell you that it is pleasant, but I will tell you that it works!

Another form of asthma is that of nervous origin. Often children will get so enraged about something that they will go purple in the face, and they will have a real attack of shortness of breath followed by wheezing. The startled parents will, of course, say, 'Oh! He has a bad attack of asthma, get the doctor quick!' The child hears that, so whenever he gets in a bad temper after he throws a fit of tantrums which comes out as a fit of asthma. He learns that if he has 'asthma' all his sins are forgotten, or forgiven, and he gets whatever he wants. Many children use 'asthma' as a weapon against parents. Often the first attack of asthma occurs in early childhood, long before the parents realise that the child can understand what they are talking about although he has not yet learned to talk himself. So, do not talk about such things in front of small babies, and find out from your doctor whether your 'asthma sufferer' really has an organic complaint or not. If he has—cure him. If he has not, then persuade him that he hasn't by absolutely ignoring these tantrums.

Many elderly people send in letters about arthritis and about rheumatism. Well, of course, you can't cure those two complaints although you can very greatly alleviate them. To start with, no one really knows what causes arthritis. It is possible to obtain herbs which can give relief to both conditions. Herbs by the name of motherwort, bitter root, and primrose can greatly assist in overcoming rheumatisms—yes, there are different kinds of rheumatisms!—and alleviating osteo-arthritis. Probably you will not be able to obtain the herbs locally, so here you get in touch with one of the two firms mentioned.

Many cases of arthritis and rheumatism can get great alleviation by moving to a different district. It is possible that the water supply is not suitable for you. It is possible that the water has too many minerals, too many hard substances, and these are conveyed through your blood-stream to various joints where they lodge and cause pain. Many people who have not been able to move from their district have secured marked improvement by getting a water filter and filtering all water before drinking it. That takes from three to six months before you observe any really marked improvement, but it's worth it, isn't it? The cost of a little water filter really can give you great relief.

The things people ask! All about their kidneys, all about the sex life, etc., etc. But, first of all, let's deal with kidneys.

Nowadays, with the horrible artificial food and chemical preparations which are being placed upon the market in greater and greater profusion, people find that their kidneys are giving trouble. So if you have kidney trouble, the herb motherwort is of very real value. It will help by clearing out your kidneys and by making you generally much, much better.

If you have kidney stones (and you are in no doubt if you have kidney stones!) you will find that parsley piert is a truly wonderful herb. The ancient name for parsley piert was 'parsley breakstone'. This herb, which can be obtained in different forms from the sources mentioned, has the truly invaluable property of causing kidney stones to crumble and turn into a form of gravel which can be passed without surgical intervention.

You would help your kidneys enormously—and help overcome arthritic and rheumatic conditions—if you would drink a lot of barley water. Here is the best way to make barley water:

Simmer pearl barley with plenty of water until it is quite soft, then strain off the water which will be cloudy. If you want to make it more pleasant you can mix it with lemonade or orangeade made with fresh lemons or oranges (the juice and a few slivers of rind) to which you add sugar and boiling water. When you have the barley water, then flavour it with the lemon or orangeade and you will find it is very refreshing and pleasant to drink. You cannot drink too much of it, it is most beneficial.

A special note—sometimes the barley water appears bluish-pink tinged, which causes some people to think there is a defect. That is not so; if this occurs it is quite normal. Drink as much as you conveniently can of this barley water, and in a surprisingly short time you will find that your kidneys are much better and that you really feel better. At the same time as you are having barley water treatment, avoid white of egg. The yolks can be taken, but avoid the white of the egg, you are better off without that in any case.

Many people nowadays have nerve troubles. The press of civilisation, the constant bustling to and fro, and all the discordant noises to which we are subjected, fray the nerves, cause headaches, cause a feeling of tension and frustration. Well, there is no need to let it go on, you know, because an exceptionally fine herb is that known as valerian. It varies a bit in name in different parts of the world, so the Latin name is *cypripedium pubescens*. It is known as 'the nerve medicine'. It has a most wonderful effect upon the mental and nervous system. If you are irritable and have a deep-seated restlessness, then you should combine valerian with passiflora.

These two herbs combined will help those who suffer from insomnia. Take a dose of the tincture, depending on your state, from five to sixty drops. This is a pair of herbs which will be of great assistance in calming the alcoholic. Give him a good dose of the stuff and it will calm him down quite a lot, and if you have menstrual pain, well, take a dose as well and it will ease your pain.

I am often often asked about diabetes. Well, if a person has a diabetic condition they must adhere to the treatment prescribed by their doctor, usually that messy insulin stuff. But you can get relief from the herb buchu. As it varies in different parts of the world, here is the Latin name: *barosma crenata*. Its action is to remove gravel which is caused by uric acid. Gentlemen will also be interested to know that this is a very beneficial treatment for chronic prostatic difficulties, when they are waiting to have an operation, or when they have refused to have an operation.

We have already dealt with constipation in another chapter. But there are so many ways of treating constipation, and I am going to put it to you that you should keep on herbal treatment for constipation. Herbs are natural, herbs help, whereas if you are going to use some of these fearsome chemical preparations you are going to end up with a case of severe internal inflammation. Try cascara, try syrup of figs, try senna, try anything of that type, and if you want something which works without pain but which also deserves the title of 'faith pill', then you should try the pills which Heath & Heather label '112'. They really work. But while on that subject, do not be too anxious to take some of these concentrated and powdered herbs for constipation because they really scour one out, and if you have to take the powdered concoctions make sure you don't have to go to work the next day. You may be so 'busy' that you haven't time to!

There is little point, really, in adding to our herbal comments because some herbs are common to one part of the world and are quite unknown in another. The firms mentioned obviously are out to make money, and so that they may the more easily do that they have an advisory department to which you can write for information as to which of their preparations will best suit your needs. It is better to do that if you are in doubt, and it is better to deal with one firm rather than to 'shop around' for someone who may be slightly, slightly cheaper. The two firms mentioned, and in whom I have no interest, financial or otherwise, are reliable firms who can really be trusted. I am not advertising them for payment. I am giving you the names because I cannot give you the names of any reputable suppliers of the raw herbs.

So, I hope that these comments will be of some benefit to you.

People seem to have a surpassing interest in 'prophecy'. They want to know what is going to happen to where, when. I said that part of America would submerge. Yes, of course it will, but people want to know how and when. They seem to think I can tell them to ten seconds or so, but I cannot because so much depends upon Americans.

Deep under the Pacific Ocean, off the American coast, there is a very serious flaw, a fault in the Earth's crust. Consider two boards, one is just barely overlapping the other along one edge. They are safe enough provided no one gives them a shake, but when one does give a board a shake, displacement occurs, and down they both drop with a real 'clump'.

Off the coast of America this fault in the seabed is such that one edge is just barely latching on to another, and an earthquake could dislodge the upper edge and cause it to slide down, giving a quite unpleasant tilt to the nearby American coastline, stretching along the Pacific Coast and affecting from Florida to New York. An earthquake could do it.

Away out in the Nevada Desert, American scientists who should know better are detonating atom bombs in the earth. They are causing earth tremors. Now, I cannot forecast when some particularly moronic scientist will detonate a bigger-than-intended bomb and shake the fault loose. If he does, he might find his feet getting wet. But this will occur eventually. It may not occur for five years, or fifty years. The probabilities are that it will be some time within the two limits, that is between five and fifty, but these are things which cannot accurately be forecast because the difference between five and fifty in Earth time is so infinitesimal in greater time that one would have to have a whole string of noughts following a decimal point. The probabilities are, though, that if Americans keep on meddling with atom bombs about which they know nothing, they will do immense damage to the whole structure of the world.

If Americans want to be safe they should move to higher ground, particularly round about the Rockies. It must also be understood that the American authorities are well aware of the dangers in this fault, but America is a politically influenced country, and the California area is a very wealthy area indeed. There are some fantastically rich exploiters of land development, and if the Government should quite reasonably declare that certain areas are not fit for habitation because of the risk of earthquakes and eventual subsidence, then the real estate speculators would raise such a howl of wrath that the American Government would topple because America is ruled by the Almighty Dollar, and a few thousand cases of human misery really do not matter to the real estate speculators or to the politicians.

Many, many geophysicists have warned the Government about the dangers in California, but they have been 'shut-up' with great effectiveness. I invite them to try to 'shut-up' me. I state emphatically that America is in grave danger on the coasts because no one is taking any thought to the future. No doubt there will be a nice Relief Fund for those still alive, but if some of these detonations in the Nevada Desert could be stopped now, then a Relief Fund later would not be required.

In the meantime I can only advise people to move to higher land when possible. Make a plan to move about five years from now, and hope that the earthquake won't occur for another fifty. In connection with this, many, many experts are stating that a great Californian earthquake is overdue. So—you have been warned.

People write to me telling me that in *Chapters of Life* I made certain prophecies, but I did not mention Australia or Africa or this or that country. No, of course I didn't! I know a lot about a lot of countries, but I did not set out to compile a guided tour of disasters or changes. I merely gave basic indications. However, let's have a look at Australia.

At present Australia is a vast continent sparsely inhabited merely on coastal regions. Australia could take a billion more people and hardly notice it, but the heart of Australia is arid. There is not much life there, there is at present no possibility of cultivating the desert areas. In many years to come the dead heart of Australia will be excavated by controlled atomic blasts. There will be a large lake made in the centre of Australia, and it will fill up quickly from great masses of fresh water, deep beneath the earth, which now has no fissure through which it may reach the surface. In years to come the interior of Australia will be flourishing indeed. When that very large lake is completed its banks will be fringed with trees and bushes imported from Brazil, and the whole climate will change as soon as the trees get rooted. For trees contribute materially to the improvement of a climate. The country will become pastoral in its interior, there will then be adequate water, and the more the trees grow, the more water there will be in the form of rains.

In the far distant future Australia, Canada, and Brazil will be the leading countries. But Australia, like Canada, has to mature first because both are immature, and even childish, and they will have much suffering because it appears that only suffering can teach. People do not learn by kindness, but only through pain and misery. Countries which have things too easy, and have too high a standard of living, just cannot, or will not, learn, and those countries have to be brought down so that by suffering and starvation, and by strikes and strife they learn the bitter lessons of life and eventually will do something to improve matters.

In the years to come Argentina will flourish. In the years to come Argentina will get back the Maldives which will later be used as a scientific research base for work in connection with U.F.O.s and the Antarctic. At present Argentina is having a very bad time indeed, but Argentinos should take heart from the fact that these are as the birth pangs of a far greater country. In years to come Argentina will be a very great, very important country indeed, with a most stable Government and a most stable economy. The Akashic Record of Probabilities indicated that Uruguay, the next door neighbour of Argentina, would have occupied that coveted position. Uruguay was going to be the Garden of South America, it, too, was going to have a lake in its interior which would vivify the arid land and make it fertile and capable of bearing lush crops. Unfortunately Uruguay is a country which has, up to now, had no suffering, and so the people of Uruguay were not able to measure up to the standard of integrity which would have been demanded. Now they are having strike after strike, and the whole country seems to be on strike, and the course of evolution does not delay just while one country settles its internal disputes. Thus, the law of Probabilities moves on, and Argentina takes the much greater place of small Uruguay.

Argentina, then, and Brazil, will be the great, great forces in South and Central America, with perhaps a preponderance of success going to Argentina because the temperature in that country is more suitable to promote human activities. The temperatures in Brazil are too equatorial to enable anyone to display any great energy.

People write to me about Africa, what do I think of Africa. Africa is a continent of turmoil, a continent enraged internally by the onslaughts of clandestine attacks by Russian and Chinese Communism, attacks which can ruin the continent's integrity. For years there will be splits and dissensions in Africa, and the Rhodesia of today, with its hatred of everything and everybody, will be swept away. In later years the whole of Africa will revert to its original status of 'the Black Continent'. It will be ruled by coloured people, it will be inhabited by coloured people, and any white person there will be there on sufferance only. There will not be populated cities of white people as at present, they will all be coloured.

But even later in history the whites and the blacks will get together again, but on a more amicable basis, and eventually as I have said in other books—there will be but one colour upon the Earth which will be known as the 'Race of Tan'.

CHAPTER EIGHT

'WELL,' said the Old Man, attempting to straighten out some of the kinks in his back and wishing that wheelchairs weren't so horribly uncomfortable, 'here is another chapter finished. Are you going to read it and see what you think?'

For some time there was silence, broken only by the sound of rustling papers. Then, at last, came the noise of a bundle of papers being thumped down on a table.

'But!' said Mrs. Old Man, 'you said you were going to mention a cure for toothache—you know a lot of people have asked about these things so why not tell them how to get rid of toothache?'

The Old Man sighed, and said, 'If people have got things wrong with their teeth the only cure is to have the wretched tooth out. I never did believe in silly things like fillings.'

Mrs. Old Man sniggered to herself, and replied, 'No, but you don't have any teeth either, or at least, none worth mentioning!'

The Old Man looked a bit glum as he felt the few remaining teeth with his tongue. 'Still,' he thought, 'there are no fillings among them, and I would have had more if I hadn't had my jaw smashed so badly.' Aloud he said, 'All right! Let's tell them something about how to cure toothache.'

Modern science (of course, that should be modern MEDICAL science) has not been able to improve upon

Nature's remedy for toothache. Modern medical science often prescribes an entirely artificial substance which has the most unfortunate vice of 'sensitising' a person against it. As it seems to me to be an invention of the Devil I will not mention its name, but there is one quite infallible natural cure for toothache.

Go to your drugstore and obtain a small bottle of oil of cloves, and then, when you get home, get a little ball of cotton wool and put a drop or two of oil of cloves on it. Gently rub the gum surrounding the offending tooth with the oil of cloves, and if the tooth has a cavity put a small amount of cotton wool, soaked in oil of cloves, so that it rests in the cavity. Within seconds your toothache will stop.

You should obtain the best grade of oil of cloves that you can, because the better the grade—the more unadulterated—the quicker the relief.

Old country people often keep a few cooking cloves in a jar, and at the first sign of toothache they put a clove on the offending tooth and bite down so that the clove is crushed and the oil inside covers the tooth. This is one of the oldest, and still one of the most modern, cures for toothache.

No matter that this is very efficient, you still need to go to your dentist to find out what really caused the toothache, because you can't keep on dunking a bad tooth in oil of cloves, can you? The best thing is to have the wretched thing out! Incidentally, I always wonder why dental treatment is such a brutal affair. I have never yet had any painless dental treatment, and it does seem to be an area which could do with a lot of research. If I had a lot of money, and so could get my auric machine going, dentists would be able to see much more clearly what is wrong with teeth, and how to get them out painlessly. What I had visualised was a thing like an instant-photograph camera which would take a photograph of the aura of a person so that anyone could see the colours. It is the colours of the aura which are important, you know. The brightness of the colours and their particular striations. If one looks at an aura, and one sees the colour of a disease, then, given suitable apparatus, it would be quite possible to cure the disease before it really got a hold. One would cure it by applying the necessary contra-colours which would change the 'degraded' colour of the illness, and so, by sympathetic reaction, the person would be cured from the aura to the physical body.

This is not a wild pipe-dream. It is a thing which really works. It is a thing which doctors should investigate. Unfortunately medical treatment is a hundred years or so behind the times, and if doctors would only get down to business and investigate new ideas instead of saying, 'That is impossible, Aristotle did not teach it,' then, no doubt, people would not suffer pain so much.

For those who desire to experiment with the aura—and who have some money—let them try buying one of those reasonably cheap television cameras, and connect it to a television set. The camera should be set to receive and transmit much higher frequencies (that is, a higher part of the spectrum) than is usual for pictures. And if the adjustment is carried out correctly the onlookers can see a fuzzy reproduction of a human body with various grey streaks and lines and sworls around the body.

If people want to experiment with a camera, and they have some knowledge of chemistry, it is possible to make sensitive material which can record a much higher frequency than that normally used in orthodox photographic work. This also works because I have taken pictures of the human aura, and I have destroyed such pictures because it gets utterly monotonous when some scientist says that such things 'cannot be, therefore the pictures must be fakes'. A scientist (that should be in quotes!) will say this even when a picture has been produced in front of him, he still thinks there is some trick somewhere, and it does appear to me that the world is not yet ready for auric photography. It needs to have the 'scientific geniuses' educated for a few years more.

Sight, and sound, and touch are very interesting subjects, you know. They are all part of the same spectrum of vibration. Do you ever stop to think when touch becomes sight or sound?

If you are touching a thing you get a very crude vibration which impresses that part of your body with which it is in contact that here is a subject of some particular composition, that is, density. You can also see such a thing. But then, do you realise that you cannot see a sound wave, nor can you hear the thing which you see. If we go from our touch point of view upwards on the scale of the spectrum, we hear a sound. That sound may be of a low note, that is almost on the touch scale, or it may be a high note which is almost into the sight scale. When your ears fail to respond to certain vibrations because they have gone too high, then your sight takes over. You may, for example, see a dull red. But, just think about sight in your next meditation.

When you see a thing you do not touch that thing. It may be in a glass bottle, it may be billions of miles away in space. But yet the thing which you see is touching you or you would not be able to perceive it. You can only see an article when that article is vibrating so much that it is continually throwing off particles of itself and generating vibrations which cross space and everything else to reach you. But these vibrations are so frail—so weak—that even a sheet of black paper can cut them out, while the coarse vibrations of sound can penetrate even a stone wall.

One could say that this life and the astral life are represented in this manner. The coarse vibrations of sound would represent life on Earth, but the finer and higher vibrations of sight would represent the astral.

There are many senses available to us in the astral which we do not even know about when in the physical. People write to me and they ask how is it possible for a fourth dimensional person to—well, as an illustration—drop a stone into one's living room. I think the person who wrote had just read an account in a newspaper about a haunted house wherein stones were thrown into locked rooms. The answer to that is that in the third dimensional world of the flesh we are only able to perceive in the dimensions of the flesh, and if there was an opening somewhere else, the flesh body's eyes would not be able to perceive it.

Let us assume that humans can only look down, or they are two dimensional. So, as they can only look down they cannot see the ceiling above. But if a person outside the room can perceive that there is no ceiling there, then that person can easily toss a brick in to the person who cannot look up. That is rather a crude way of explaining it, but what really happens is that every room, or everything on Earth, has another opening, another aperture, which humans on Earth cannot perceive because they lack the necessary organ with which to perceive that dimension. Yet a person who is in a fourth dimensional world can make use of that opening and pass things through it into what, to the third dimensional inhabitant, is a closed space.

This type of 'joke' is often played by lower entities who like to pose as poltergeists.

We must not forget the lady who wrote in and asked me if I could explain in simple terms the nature of telepathy. She had read my other books, but apparently this subject of telepathy had her completely baffled. Let's see what we can do, shall we?

Even scientists now agree that the brain generates electricity. There are medical procedures in which brain-waves are charted. A special apparatus is placed on the head, and four squiggly lines indicate four different levels of thought. For some strange reason these four squiggly lines are given Greek names, which doesn't concern us at all. But the brain generates electricity, and the electricity varies according to what one is thinking in much the same way as if when one is speaking into a microphone, the words generate a current which continuously varies in intensity according to what is being said. In a tape recorder, for example, one speaks and one's speech impresses minute magnetic currents on a specially prepared tape. Afterwards, when the tape is played back, one obtains a reproduction of the original speech. The human brain generates an electric current which other brains can pick up, in much the same way as the tape on a tape recorder picks up the minute impulses from voice vibrations which are transferred to electric impulses.

When you think, you broadcast your thoughts. Most people are immune to the noise of the thoughts of other people, and fortunately so because everyone is thinking something all the time, and unless people were immune to that continuous, non-stop, never-ending noise, one would go 'quite round the bend'. By special training, or by a fluke of Nature, one can tune-in to thoughts, because, as our brains generate electricity, so they are able to receive electric impressions. It is a form of telepathy which keeps the body in touch with the Overself, the telepathy in this instance being a very special ultra high frequency current going from the brain of the flesh body, by way of the Silver Cord, and on to the Overself.

But, to reply in the simplest possible terms to the question, 'How does telepathy work?' it is necessary only to say that every brain acts as a radio transmitter and radio receiver, and if you knew how to switch on your receiver you would be inundated with everybody else's thoughts. You can pick up the thoughts of those with whom you are compatible far more easily than you can pick up the thoughts of those with whom you are not compatible. And a good exercise is to 'guess' what a person whom you know well is going to say next. If you 'guess' for some time, you will soon discover that your successes are far outstripping the laws of chance, and when you begin to realise that you are well on the way to telepathic communication with the person with whom you are compatible. Here again, it is a matter which needs practice and patience, and when you are telepathic you will wish you were not, because life will be a constant babble, what with humans and animals all the time talking to each other.

CHAPTER NINE

OUTSIDE the window the noise and the clamour were continuous. High-speed pneumatic hammers were drilling holes many feet into the old rock, a rock which used to be the site of many fine old houses. In years gone by the wives of sea captains lived here, and kept their nightly vigil of the sea, waiting for their men to return home, home to the haven of the harbour with the ever-burning light beckoning from the house windows. One fine old house, towering above the others, had stood proud for years, and in its declining days the ghost of the old lady who had watched, and watched in vain, for the return of her beloved husband, had become well known. Nightly she stood at the port side window, with her hands holding aside the drapes so that she could see the more clearly. Night after night, in ghostly outline, she stood there, peering, peering, seeking the man who never came back to her, the man whose body lay beneath the surface of the ocean a thousand miles from home.

Now the house was down, demolished. The whole street of houses was down, and the voracious drills and hammers were biting at the living rock, tearing it up in great chunks to make way for the progress of civilisation. Here would be a great road, an artery of the community. A road spanning the city, spanning, too, the river, linking one side to the other by a new bridge. The clamour was continuous. Immense bulldozers shoved vast piles of rock and earth, steam shovels gouged into the soil, trucks rattled and roared at all hours of the day and night. There was the shouting of men, and the barking of dogs, and peace had fled long ago.

The Old Man bent over the letters from readers, and set aside the last one. Mrs. Old Man looked up, perhaps with a sigh of relief to see that work was coming to an end. Then she rose to feed the Little Girl Cats who had come bustling in to say that it was their teatime, and could they have their food in a hurry, please, because they had thought a lot and were very hungry. So Mrs. Old Man went off with a cat on each side.

The Old Man turned to Buttercup, Buttercup who, in Spanish, was mis-named Amapola. 'Buttercup,' said the Old Man, 'it doesn't matter that there has been a mail strike, we've done some good work in answering all these queries, haven't we?'

Buttercup looked pleased to think that work was coming to an end for another day, 'You only started this fourteen days ago,' she said, 'and now the book is finished in record time.'

'Yes,' replied the Old Man, 'but you've typed seven thousand words a day, haven't you? And now we've come to an end.'

Buttercup smiled with pleasure at the thought. 'Well, in that case I will just type

THE END'

replied Buttercup.

'KINDNESS TO PUBLISHERS' DEPARTMENT

THROUGHOUT the years since *The Third Eye* first appeared I have had a tremendous amount of mail, and up to the present I have always answered that mail. Now I have to say that I am no longer able to reply to any mail at all unless adequate return postage is enclosed. So please do NOT send letters to my Publisher for forwarding to me because I have asked my Publisher not to forward any letters.

People forget that they pay for a BOOK, and NOT a lifetime of free post-paid advisory service. Publishers are PUBLISHERS—not a letter forwarding service.

I have letters from all over the world, even from well behind the Iron Curtain, but not one in several thousand people encloses return postage, and the cost is so much that I can no longer undertake replies.

People ask such peculiar things, too. Here are just some:

There was a very desperate letter from Australia which reached me when I was in Ireland. The matter was (apparently) truly urgent, so at my own expense I sent a cable to Australia, and I did not even receive a note of thanks.

A certain gentleman in the U.S.A. wrote me a letter DEMANDING that I should immediately write a thesis for him and send it by return airmail. He wanted to use it as his thesis to obtain a Doctorate in Oriental Philosophy. Of course he did not enclose any postage, it was merely a somewhat threatening demand!

An Englishman wrote me a very, very haughty letter in the third person, demanding my credentials, because if they were completely satisfactory to this person he would consider placing himself under my tuition provided that there would be no charge for it. In other words, I was supposed to be honoured. (I do not think he would like my reply!)

Another one wrote to me and said that if I 'and my chums' would come from Tibet and cluster around his bed in the astral at night then he would be able to feel more happy about astral travelling.

Other people write to me and ask me everything from high esoteric things (which I can answer if I want to) to how to keep hens and one's husband! People also consider that they should write to me just whenever they think they should, and they get offensive if I do not reply by return airmail.

I will ask you NOT to bother my Publishers, in fact I have asked them not to send on any letters to me because they are in business as Publishers. For those who really do need an answer (although I do not invite letters) I have an accommodation address. It is:

>   Dr. T. Lobsang Rampa
>   BM/TLR,
>   London W.C.1., England.

I do not guarantee any reply, and if you use this address you will have to provide very adequate postage because the letters will be forwarded to me and I shall have to pay, so I shall not be in a sweet enough mood to reply unless you have made my expense your expense. For example, it will cost me a dollar at least by the time forwarding charges are paid.

Dr. Rampa's Tranquilliser Touch-Stones

You are interested in the Higher Sciences or you would not be reading this book. Have you considered how your tranquillity can be nourished by a Rampa-Touch-Stone? On page 123 in *Wisdom of the Ancients* you can read about these Touch-Stones. They are available with simple instructions

---

AN INSTRUCTION RECORD ON MEDITATION

A large number of people wrote to Lobsang Rampa demanding a record about Meditation, so at last he has made the only special, fully authentic recording by him. Tells you how to meditate, shows you how easy it is, places peace, harmony and inner contentment within YOUR reach. Rampa-Touch-Stones Ltd. can supply this 12" record AND THE TRANQUILLISER TOUCH STONE ANYWHERE at the prices below AIRMAIL FREE.

Price List	Record	Tranquilliser Touch-Stones	
Australia	4	4.20	dollars
Austria	110	120	schillings
Belgium	220	230	francs
Canada	5.50	5.50	dollars
Denmark	30	33.5	kroner
France	20	24	francs
Great Britain	33	37	shillings
Germany	17	18	deutsche marks
Holland	15	17	guilders
Italy	2500	2900	lires
New Zealand	4	4.20	dollars
Norway	30	32	kroner
S. Africa	3.5	3.8	rand
Sweden	20	25	kroner
U.S.A.	5	5	dollars
All other places 40 shillings or 5 dollars EACH ITEM			

Rampa-Touch-Stones Ltd.
33 Ashby Road, Loughborough, Leicestershire, England.

A SELECTION OF FINE READING AVAILABLE IN CORGI BOOKS

Novels

☐	552 08457 3	ANOTHER COUNTRY	*James Baldwin* 6/-
☐	552 08351 8	TELL ME HOW LONG THE TRAIN'S BEEN GONE	*James Baldwin* 7/-
☐	552 07938 3	THE NAKED LUNCH	*William Burroughs* 7/6
☐	652 08370 4	MAROONED	*Martin Caidin* 6/-
☐	552 08443 3	MISS MAMMA AIMEE	*Erskine Caldwell* 5/-
☐	552 08374 7	THE BANNERS OF LOVE	*Sacha Carnegie* 7/-
☐	552 08419 0	THE FIFTEEN STREETS	*Catherine Cookson* 5/-
☐	552 08444 1	MAGGIE ROWAN	*Catherine Cookson* 6/-
☐	552 08183 3	BOYS AND GIRLS TOGETHER	*William Goldman* 7/6
☐	552 07968 5	THE WELL OF LONELINESS	*Radclyffe Hall* 7/6
☐	552 08125 6	CATCH-22	*Joseph Heller* 7/-
☐	552 08418 2	THE CLINIC	*James Kerr* 7/-
☐	552 08416 6	VAIL D'ALVERY	*Frances Parkinson Keyes* 7/-
☐	552 08415 8	THE RIVER ROAD	*Frances Parkinson Keyes* 6/-
☐	552 08420 4	ANGELS IN THE SNOW	*Derek Lambert* 7/-
☐	552 08393 3	WHITE HELL OF PITY	*Norah Lofts* 5/-
☐	552 08332 1	I MET A GIPSY	*Norah Lofts* 4/-
☐	552 08442 5	THE AU PAIR BOY	*Andrew McCall* 6/-
☐	552 08002 0	MY SISTER, MY BRIDE	*Edwina Mark* 5/-
☐	552 08352 6	THE WAYWARD FLESH	*Nan Maynard* 5/-
☐	552 08402 2	THE FIRES OF SPRING	*James A. Michener* 8/-
☐	552 08406 9	RETURN TO PARADISE	*James A. Michener* 6/-
☐	552 08312 7	THE SAVAGE EARTH	*Helga Moray* 5/-
☐	552 08445 X	THE PASSION PLAYERS	*Edmund Murray* 7/-
☐	552 08124 9	LOLITA	*Vladimir Nabokov* 6/-
☐	552 07954 5	RUN FOR THE TREES	*James Rand* 7/-
☐	552 08392 5	SOMETHING OF VALUE	*Robert Ruark* 8/-
☐	552 08372 0	LAST EXIT TO BROOKLYN	*Hubert Selby, Jr.* 10/-
☐	552 08459 X	THE PASTURES OF HEAVEN	*John Steinbeck* 4/-
☐	552 07807 7	VALLEY OF THE DOLLS	*Jacqueline Susann* 7/6
☐	552 08013 6	THE EXHIBITIONIST	*Henry Sutton* 7/6
☐	552 08217 1	THE CARETAKERS	*Dariel Telfer* 7/-
☐	552 08091 8	TOPAZ	*Leon Uris* 7/6
☐	552 08384 4	EXODUS	*Leon Uris* 8/-
☐	552 08446 8	A MISTRESS FOR THE VALOIS	*Julia Watson* 5/-
☐	552 08437 9	WAIT FOR TOMORROW	*Robert Wilder* 7/-
☐	552 08438 7	THE SUN IS MY SHADOW	*Robert Wilder* 6/-
☐	552 08073 X	THE PRACTICE	*Stanley Winchester* 7/6
☐	552 08391 7	MEN WITH KNIVES	*Stanley Winchester* 7/-
☐	552 07116 1	FOREVER AMBER Vol. I	*Kathleen Winsor* 5/-
☐	552 07117 X	FOREVER AMBER Vol. II	*Kathleen Winsor* 5/-

War

☐	552 08410 7	THE DEEP SIX	*Martin Dibner* 6/-
☐	552 08409 3	THE SEA OUR SHIELD	*Captain W. R. Fell* 7/-
☐	552 08447 6	COMMAND DECISION	*William Wister Haines* 5/-
☐	552 08315 1	THE SAVAGES	*Ronald Hardy* 6/-

All these books are available at your book shop or newsagent; or can be ordered direct from the publisher. Just tick the titles you want and fill in the form below.

CORGI BOOKS. Cash Sales Department, P.O. Box 11, Falmouth, Cornwall.

Please send cheque or postal order. No currency, and allow 6d. per book to cover the cost of postage and packing in U.K., 9d. per copy overseas.

NAME ....

ADDRESS ....

(JUNE '70) ....